W9-CXC-059

PLACE IN RETURN BOX to remove this checkout from your record.
TO AVOID FINES return on or before date due.

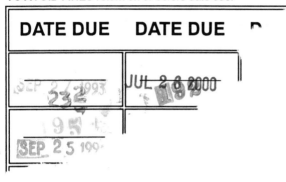

DATE DUE	DATE DUE	D
SEP 2 7 1993 232 19 ‡ SEP 2 5 199‡	JUL 2 6 2000 ‡ 199‡	

THE DIARY OF SØREN KIERKEGAARD

THE DIARY
OF
SØREN
KIERKEGAARD

Translated from the Danish by Gerda M. Andersen

Edited by Peter P. Rohde

PHILOSOPHICAL LIBRARY
New York

After my death no one shall find in my papers (that is my consolation) the slightest enlightenment on what fundamentally filled my life, nor find the writing in my inmost being that explains everything and often makes what the world would call trifles into vastly important events to me and [vice versa] what I regard as insignificant—when I eliminate the secret note that explains it.

Translated from the Danish by Gerda M. Andersen

Library of Congress Catalogue Card Number 60-13649

Copyright, 1960, by Philosophical Library, Inc.
15 East 40th Street, New York 16, N. Y.

Type set by The Polyglot Press
Printed in the United States of America

CONTENTS

PREFACE

The luckless reader who sets out on his own to find his way in Kierkegaard's vast, and vastly demanding, works, runs the risk of losing his way and finally of losing his courage. Kierkegaard himself, if he had been asked, would no doubt have advised the beginner to go straight to his *Edifying Discourses,* which the author issued under his own name and offered the public with his right hand, whereas he offered the pseudonymous writings with his left, as it were. But not everyone is able to follow this advice, and the majority of the many interested readers all over the world who delve into the works of the Danish thinker and religious personality undoubtedly feel more drawn to the pseudonymous writings. Among these the novels *Either-Or* and *Stages on Life's Way* are easiest of access, but so voluminous that they hardly qualify as introductory fare for the study of the philosopher, especially not in schools (and making cuts in them would be tantamount to mutilation). On the other hand, the smaller books, such as *Repetition, Fear and Trembling, The Concept of Dread* and *The Sickness unto Death,* in their concentrated and thought-laden presentation, are wholly inaccessible to students who have not yet worked their way into the author's special way of expressing himself and his world of ideas so alien to our contemporary age. These considerations might well be the reason why so few have had sufficient courage to experiment with Kierkegaard in the classroom.

However, there is another possible approach. Kierkegaard's writings included a great deal more than his published works of some 5000 pages. In addition there were his journals, almost twice as voluminous; it was his wont to confide himself day and night to these journals, which form an indispensable accompaniment to the body of his work. They furnish the human background for its creation, permit us to witness this very creation. They confront us with the thinker as he existed, and etch a life in glimpses which, though fragmentary, constitute something else and more than a biography, in fact something unique in world literature. It is precisely their fragmentary character that dispenses us from the obligation which the finished works place upon us, viz. to respect their wholeness—for it is non-existent. However, from their 8,000 to 10,000 pages it is possible to distil some one hundred and fifty pages that contain the true essence —that is, if the editor has been successful in his selection.

For Kierkegaard the journals fulfilled a special function. For one thing, they served him as a direct release from his cooped-up emotions, more numerous and more violent in him than in most other persons, partly because his inborn nature was extremely reserved and *not able* to confide in others, partly because in his works he hid from his readers behind pseudonyms, *not wanting* to confide in anyone. That had something to do with his conviction that one must not try to *indoctrinate*, but—like Socrates—present his opinions indirectly, so that those to whom he addressed himself should not fall victim to his influence, but be stimulated to independent thinking. Only thus would they be able to make the free choice which to him appeared as the absolute *sine qua non* of Christianity.

A psychologist would presumably interpret this as evidence of Kierkegaard's introversion and disinclination to enter into direct contact with human beings, and explain it on the basis of impressions K. received in his childhood. We shall abstain from any attempt at distinguishing in favor of one or the other viewpoint; still, it is not amiss to hint that no one understood Kierkegaard's clinical case better than K. himself, and no one has described its presuppositions more succinctly.

A second function of the journals was that in them Kierkegaard could speak out quite deliberately, express his opinions without circumlocution. It is true that he was the only one to derive any satisfaction from that; still, here and there certain entries show that often enough he was giving some thought to the prospect that after his death the journals might in some way become accessible to a wider public. That was why he carefully preserved every scrap of paper he had written, but also took care that certain things which he had scribbled down in the heat of passion were later removed. As a result there are frequent gaps in the journals, and these gaps always occur where he had revealed something about what he called the secret of his life, the secret note. Such maneuvers, however, only would make sense if he had in mind that the journals at some future time would be seen by others. It consoled him to think that after he had passed away readers would receive a direct communication from him in which, without beating around the bush, he clarified the motives for his actions, offered a key to the understanding of his life, as well as of his works, even though he remained unable to break through his reserve to the point where he could deliver up the key to the innermost chamber of the vast structure built around his heart, that would ensure *complete* understanding.

But even with this reservation, the journals constitute a natural introduction to Kierkegaard's works. In them he expresses in simple words what one may find expressed in his works in more mystifying, but also in more philosophically demanding, terms. The present selection aims at emphasizing the introductory character of the journals by including and illuminating as many entries as possible on the concepts and ideas which Kierkegaard handled in his works with the same ease as a Chinese juggler balancing his jars and poles on his head, nose, toes and fingers. This has necessitated more detailed and more numerous notes[1] than the reader (presumably) and the editor (certainly) care for. But it was unavoidable. Undeniably, the terminology and concepts of the philosophical age are not directly accessible to twentieth-century youngsters. However, it might prove well worth while to toil for some hours over these unaccustomed phenomena. It was the *forte* of that

[1] *Translator's note*: Words and passages in the text which are further elucidated by editorial notes in the Appendix have been marked by an asterisk (*). Annotations by the editor of the Danish edition are indicated by a dagger (†).

age that it was well versed in the basic concepts, in the categories. We are not. This is one of the things we may learn from Kierkegaard.

The present selection follows *in the main* a chronological plan. It is based on the events which marked the course of Kierkegaard's life like milestones along a highway: his relations with his father; the influence of the author Poul Møller; his engagement; the *Corsair* episode with editor Meïr Aaron Goldschmidt; the troubled times around 1848, and Kierkegaard's attack on the Church. However, included in the several sections are pieces written at a later date, but throwing light on the episodes under review; the chronological framework is also broken by four large sections of a more systematic character: one on Kierkegaard's writing over the years, one on his philosophical ideas, one on Christianity, and one on the Christian Church and Congregation. Within the chronological order the four sections are placed in such a way that they do not perhaps, after all, break it so much as point to the direction Kierkegaard's life was taking.

The entries start with a section entitled "Life-Mood," which the reader is asked to peruse in one sitting and without paying too much attention to impeding comments. In that way he cannot help having his ear attuned to the grand general rhythm of Kierkegaard's life and art, and it would be a good thing if the feel of the rhythm lingered on in the reader's mind later when he tackles the journals in a more analytical and pedestrian manner. Thus there is hope that he will avoid being swamped by innumerable troublesome details.

In this selection Kierkegaard's orthography and punctuation are reproduced exactly as he wrote.[2] He himself admitted that his orthography was very haphazard, partly because he never bothered about systematic orthography, being unable to take any real interest in this aspect of writing, partly because he paid no heed to trifles and wrote very rapidly.

His punctuation in the journals was also very casual, but if the reader follows Kierkegaard's viewpoints he will easily sense the rhythmic flight and the shades of opinion K. seeks to emphasize by his punctuation.[3] Haphazard faults that would be intolerable in the edited writings lend the journal-entries an intimate charm, and since no one can be sure of drawing the right line of demarcation between what is deliberate and what is slipshod, he must abstain from attempts at improvement based on critical guesswork.

For advice and constructive criticism the editor wishes to thank Professor F. J. Billeskov Jansen, Headmaster Arne Olesen, Lecturer J. A. Bundgaard, Secondary-School-Teacher Niels Ferlov, Librarian Erik Dal and—not least—Alf Henriques, Ph.D., who has followed with unabating interest the development of this small book from its very beginning.

Peter P. Rohde

---

[2] *Translator's note*: These characteristics do not always come through in the English translation.

[3] *Translator's note*: It has not been possible to reproduce fully the peculiarities of Kierkegaard's punctuation in translation.

I

LIFE MOOD

1.   *1836.*

I have just returned from a party of which I was the life and soul; witty banter flowed from my lips, everyone laughed and admired me—but I came away, indeed that dash should be as long as the radii of the earth's orbit———————————wanting to shoot myself.

2.   *1836.*

Death and Damnation, I can dissociate from everything else but my own self; I can't even forget myself when I am asleep.

3.

An ambulant musician played the minuet from Don Giovanni on some kind of reed-pipe (I couldn't see what it was as he was in the next courtyard), and the druggist was pounding medicine with his pestle, and the maid was scouring in the yard,† etc., and they noticed nothing and maybe the piper didn't either, and I felt such well-being.   June 10, 1836.

† and the groom curried his horse and beat off the curry-comb against the curb, and from another part of town came the distant cry of a shrimp vender.

4.   *1837.*

There are many people who arrive at the result of
their lives like schoolboys; they cheat their teacher
by copying the answer from the key in the arithmetic-
book, without bothering to do the sums themselves.

January 17, 1837.

5.   *1837.*

The path we all must take—across the Bridge of Sighs*
into eternity.

6.   *1837.*

It is those petty teasings that embitter life so much.
I will gladly struggle on in the face of a gale, my
veins almost bursting; but a wind that blows a speck
of dust into my eyes can vex me to such an extent
that I stamp my foot.

These petty teasings are as if a man wanted to en-
gage in a great work, a great enterprise on which his
own life and the lives of many others depended—and
then a gadfly settled on his nose.

7.   *1837.*

One thought chases the next; no sooner have I thought
it and am about to write it down than a new one
comes along—hold it, grasp it—Madness—Insanity!

8.   *1837.*

Altogether I hate these pseudo-scholars—how often at
a party have I not deliberately sat down by some
elderly spinster-lady who feeds on repeating family
news, and with the utmost gravity listened to her
chatter.

9. *1837.*

I prefer talking with old persons of the female sex who peddle family gossip; next, with the insane—and last, with very sensible people.

10. *1837.*

I can't bother to do anything whatsover;* I can't bother to walk—the effort is too great; I can't bother to lie down, for either I would lie too long, and I can't bother to do that, or I would get up at once, and I can't bother to do that either—I can't bother to go horseback-riding—the exercise is too strenuous for my apathy; all I can bother to do is ride in a carriage, comfortably, and, while being evenly rocked, let a multitude of objects glide past me, lingering over each lovely bit of scenery only to savor my languor—my thoughts and notions are as sterile as a eunuch's heat—in vain I seek something that might enliven me—not even the pithy language of the Middle Ages can overcome the void that pervades my being. Now I realize in truth what is meant by the saying about Christ's words, that they are life and spirit*—in brief: I can't bother to write what I have just written, and I can't bother to blot it out.

11. *1837.*

Again there is new life in Amager Square¹ and the colorful, flowery coverlet of folk-life is spread over it. Last night at midnight an individual in shabby clothes was seized because, as the night-watchman

¹ *Translator's note:* A market in the center of Copenhagen, principally a flower-market.

said, he had heaped gross abuse on some persons, but
the night-watchman who should report such things
had not seen it, and the culprit was beaten—unjustly
—it is believed—and no one made a complaint—no
one knows anything about it. Today life goes on as
usual—and this is merely Amager Square—what is
that compared to Denmark, Europe, the world?

12.

"Love Thy neighbor as Thyself," say the Philistine
bourgeois whereby these well-raised children and now
useful members of the state—who are very susceptible
to any passing emotional influenza—mean, partly, that
if someone asks for a pair of snuffers, even though
they be quite far from that person, they shall say
"certainly," get up, and hand the snuffers to the person assuring same that "it is a pleasure"; partly, that
one must remember to pay the obligatory calls of
condolence. But they have never known what it
means that the whole world turns its back on them,
as of course the shoal of society-herring among which
they live never will permit such a contingency to
arise, and when a time comes when serious help is
required from them, common sense of course will
tell them that the person who needs them sorely, but
presumably never will be in a position to help them
in return, is *not* their "neighbor."   July 18, 1837.

13.

The Philistine bourgeois* always skip a certain element in life, and that becomes the cause of their
parodic relation to those above them. To them "morality" ranks highest; it is much more important than

intelligence; they never have felt any enthusiasm for the Great, the Gifted, whether deviating from the norm or not. Their *morals* constitute a brief summary of various police-regulations posters; for them the most important is to be useful members of the state and to hold forth evenings in their club; they never have felt nostalgia for something mysterious, for something far-away, never sensed the deeply rewarding feeling in being nothing at all, in strolling out of town by the North Gate with 4 pennies in one's pocket and carrying a slender bamboo cane; they have no inkling of that life-philosophy (adopted by a Gnostic sect,* you know) which aimed at getting to know the world by way of sin—yet they too say that one must sow one's wild oats in youth ("wer niemals hat ein Rausch gehabt, er ist kein braver Mensch");[1] they never had a glimpse of the underlying idea, when, through the hidden, secret door—opened in all its horror only through a flash of precognition—one penetrates into the dark realm of sighs—when one sees the crushed victims of seduction and ensnarement and the icy cold of the tempter.

July 14, 1837.

14.   *1838*.

Man almost never avails himself of his freedoms, freedom of thought, for instance; instead he demands freedom of speech.*

15.   *1837*.

Each person takes his revenge on the world. Mine

[1] *Translator's note:* "Who never was drunk is not a right good fellow."

consists in carrying my grief and anguish deeply embedded within myself, while my laughter entertains
all. If I see somebody suffer I sympathize with him,
console him to the best of my ability, and listen to
him quietly when he assures me that *I* am fortunate.
If I can keep this up to the day of my death I shall
have had my revenge.

16.

The other day I was sitting in a strange mood, sunk
into myself (the way an old ruin might feel) and
gradually losing myself and my Ego in a kind of
pantheistic disintegration. I was reading an old ballad* (edited by Sneedorf-Birch) telling about a girl
waiting for her lover on a Saturday night; but he did
not come—and she went to bed "and wept so bitterly";
she got up "and wept so bitterly," and suddenly the
scene expanded in my mind: I saw the Jutland heath
in its indescribable loneliness, with its solitary sky-
lark—then one generation after the other rose up, and
all their maidens sang for me and wept so bitterly,
and sank back into their graves again, and I wept
with them.

Strange to say, my imagination works best when I
am sitting by myself in a big gathering where chatter
and noise provide a substratum for my will to cling
to its object; without such surroundings it bleeds to
death in the unnerving embrace of a vague idea.

December 30, 1937.

17.   *1837*.

How awful it would be on Judgment Day when all
souls return to life again—then to stand completely
alone, alone and *unknown* to All, All.

18.

All of existence intimidates me, from the tiniest fly
to the enigmas of incarnation;* as a whole it is inexplicable, my own self most of all; all of existence
is pestiferous, my own self most of all. Great is my
grief, limitless; no one knows it except God in Heav-
en, and he will not comfort me; no one can comfort
me save God in Heaven, and he will not have mercy
upon me—young man, youth, you who still stand at
the beginning of the road, if you have lost your way,
turn back, oh, turn back to God, and through his
teaching you will save your youth, strengthened for
the deeds of manhood. And you shall never know
what he must suffer who, having wasted the strength
and courage of his young days in rebelling against
Him, now, unnerved and helpless, must begin a
retreat through ruined lands and ravaged regions,
surrounded on all sides by the abomination of desola-
tion, by gutted cities and smoking ruins of hope deceived, of prosperity stamped out and palmy days
gone forever, a retreat slow as an evil year, long as
eternity, monotonously interrupted by the constantly
repeated plaint: "I have no pleasure in them [these
days]."*

May 12, 1839.

19.

At present my life can almost be likened to what a
chess-piece in a game must feel when the opponent
says: This piece is not to be touched—like an idle
onlooker; for my hour has not yet struck.

May 21, 1839.

20.*   *1840.*

There are no people I wish so hard would fall, or
that Knippel Bridge [in Copenhagen] might be raised
in their faces, etc., than those bustling businessmen
who have so infinitely much they *must* accomplish in
the world, instead of, like the rest of us, when Knippel Bridge is raised, finding it a good opportunity for
musing ...

21.   *1841.*

Besides my numerous circle of acquaintances with
whom, by and large, I maintain very superficial relations, I have one close confidant—my melancholy—
and in the midst of my rejoicing, in the midst of my
work, she waves to me, beckons me to her side and I
go to her, even though my physical frame stays in
place; she is the most faithful mistress I have known;
what wonder then that I, on my part, must be ready
to follow her on the instant.

22.   *1841.*

... And when God wishes to bind a human being to
Him in earnest, He summons one of His most faithful servants, His trustiest messenger, Grief, and tells
him: Hurry after him, overtake him, do not budge
from his side (... and no woman can cling more
tenderly to what she loves than Grief) .

23.   *1844.*

In former days a man derived self-importance by being born noble, rich, etc.; today we have grown more
liberal, more "world-historical," now all of us derive
self-importance from being born in the 19th century

—Oh, Thou marvelous 19th century! Oh, enviable lot!

24. *1845.*
*Remark by a Humorous Individual**

"Just as a person feels most comfortable shuffling through life without being known either by His Majesty the King, Her Majesty the Queen, Her Majesty the Queen Dowager, or by His Royal Highness the Crown Prince, so, in turn, it seems to me that being known by God makes life infinitely burdensome. Wherever He is by, each half hour becomes *infinitely* important. No one can stand living like that for 60 years, no more than he can stand cramming for his final examination which, after all, involves only 3 years and is not such a terrible effort. Everything dissolves in contradiction. One moment they preach to you that you must not go about half asleep, but live your life with the highest passion of the Infinite. All right, you pull yourself together: you arrive starched and strait-laced at the parade—then you are told that you should learn to shorten your sails. What does it all mean? *am Ende* [in the end] all human beings have come equally far, and the whole thing is not worth much. It is the same as when I saw my physician recently. I complained about not feeling well. He replied: "Perhaps you drink too much coffee and do not walk enough." Three weeks later I talked to him again and said: "I really don't feel well, but now it cannot be because of my coffee-drinking, for I don't drink coffee, nor from lack of exercise, for I walk all day long." He replied: "Well, the reason must be that you don't drink coffee and

walk too much." In other words, my indisposition
remained the same, but if I drink coffee it is due to
my coffee-drinking; and if I don't take coffee my indisposition is due to my not drinking coffee. And so
with us human beings. Our whole earthly existence
is a sort of indisposition; with some the cause for it is
that they make too great an effort; in others, too little
effort, and if one inquires into the cause, the man
you ask will first say: "Do you make a great effort?"
If you answer yes, he will say: "The cause is that you
work too strenuously." If you answer no, he will say
the opposite, put his tail between his legs and slink
off. Even if somebody offered me 10 rixdollars I
would not take it upon myself to explain the enigma
of life. And, anyway, why should I? If life is an enigma, a puzzle, he who has posed it probably will come
forth in the end and offer the solution when he feels
that nobody is too eager to make a guess any longer. I
have not invented the puzzle, but in "The Liberal,"*
"The Freischutz"* as well as other papers that feature
puzzles, the solution follows in the next issue. The
distinction of being mentioned in the paper as the
person who had solved the puzzle on the same day
that the rest of us learn the solution is a matter of
indifference to me."

> (Elderly spinster or retired pen-
> sioner who solves puzzles.)

25.   *1845.*
Remark*

Like an invalid longing to throw off his bandages, so
my healthy spirit longs to throw off my body's debility (*Marginal note*: that stuffy poultice, soaked

through with sweat: the body and the body's debility) ; like a victorious general, who when his horse is hit by a bullet under him, calls out for a new horse —Oh, if my spirit's victorious health likewise dared call out: a new horse, a new body (*Marginal note*: for only the body is exhausted); like a person at sea, whose life is threatened and, when another drowning man tries to take hold of his leg, pushes him away with all his might, thus my body like a heavy weight dragging me down clings to my spirit and will end by perishing; like a steamer whose engines are too large in proportion to the vessel's construction: that is the way I suffer.

26.   1847.

Since my earliest childhood a barb of sorrow has lodged in my heart. As long as it stays I am ironic—if it is pulled out I shall die.

27.   1847.

It is an awful satire, and an epigram* on the materialism of our modern age, that nowadays the only use that can be made of solitude is imposing it as a penalty, as jail. What a difference there is between those times when, no matter how secular materialism always was, man believed in the solitude of the convent, when, in other words, solitude was revered as the highest, as the destiny of Eternity—and the present when it is detested as a curse and is used only for the punishment of criminals. Alas, what a change.

28.   1850.

It is the old story. A discovery is made—the human race triumphs; enthusiastically everything, everything is set going to perfect the discovery more and more. The human race is jubilant and worships itself. At long last there comes a halt—man pauses and asks: is this discovery really a boon, especially the extraordinary perfection of it that has been achieved! Then a new call goes out for the most eminent heads, and they torture their brains almost to madness to find safety-valves, dampers, clogs, etc. in order, if possible, to put a brake on, to prevent this matchless and matchlessly perfected discovery, the pride of the human race, from riding rough-shod over the whole world and destroying it. Consider, for instance, the invention of the printing press, perfected to a top-speed machine* sure to guarantee that no dirt or dregs remain unpublished. Consider the railways.* Consider the free constitutions,* these matchlessly perfected discoveries—the pride of the human race— which make us hanker for some Oriental despotism as offering its subjects more chance of happiness.

29.   *1851.*

Contrast

God's word was spoken (communicated only orally) by one human being, and later written down—today every prattler can have his balderdash printed in tens of thousands of copies.

According to our contemporary way of thinking one would have expected that the Lord would at least have waited to let himself be born until the art of printing had been invented, that until then the fullness of time had not arrived, and that he would then have secured one or two high-speed printing presses. Oh, what a satire on humanity that God's word was put into the world the way it was, and what a satire on humanity that the more the preaching of the Good Tidings deteriorates, the wider the circulation it receives by means of ever new inventions.

30. *1854.*
*"Nail down the Lid"**

These words are from an old hymn. Nail down the lid, that is, the coffin-lid; nail it securely, truly fast, so that—like a child who enjoys the height of bliss when it has managed to find a really good hiding-place—I may remain in peace, truly hidden.

Nail down the lid very securely—for it is not I lying in the coffin, no, what is lying there is what I yearned so infinitely to be rid of, this body of sin, this prison uniform I have been made to wear.

31. *1854.*
"Nail down the Lid"

Listen to the cry of a woman in labor at the hour of giving birth—look at the dying man's struggle at his last extremity, and then tell me whether something that begins and ends thus could be intended for enjoyment.

True, we humans do everything possible to get away as quickly as possible from those two points; we hurry as much as possible to forget the cry of birth-pangs and to change into pleasure the act of having given life to another being, And when someone is dead we hasten to say: He went to sleep gently and softly; death is a sleep, a quiet sleep—all of which we do not proffer for the sake of the deceased, since our words cannot help him in the slightest, but for our own sakes, so as not to lose our joy in life; we do it in order to have everything serve to heighten our joy in life during the interim between the birth-cry and the death-cry, between the mother's cry and the child's repetition thereof in the hour of death.

Suppose that somewhere there was a superbly magnificent hall where no effort had been spared to produce everlasting bliss and joy—but that the ascent to this hall had to be made by a noisome, dirty chicken-ladder, and it was impossible to mount it without getting loathsomely soiled, and the entrance fee had to be paid by prostituting* oneself, and when dawn neared the merriment was over, and it all ended by one being hustled out again—but all through the night nothing was spared to kindle and keep up gaiety and rejoicing!

What is reflection? Surely it means to ponder those two very questions: how did I get into this and that, and how will I get out of it again, how will it end. What is thoughtlessness? To muster everything for drowning in oblivion all about entrance and exit; to muster everything for circumventing and explaining away the questions of entrance and exit, alone and lost in the interim between the confined woman's cry and the repetition of that cry when the person then born expires in the agony of death.

II

CHILDHOOD AND YOUTH

1. FATHER AND SON

32.   *1844.*

Quiet Despair

A Story.

In his youth Dean Swift founded a lunatic asylum where he himself was placed in his old age. It is told that while there he would often look at himself in a mirror and say: Poor old man.

There were a father and a son. Both very gifted, both witty, especially the father. Probably everyone who knew their home and frequented it found them very entertaining. Mostly they debated with each other and entertained each other like two clever fellows, not like father and son. Once in a long while the father would look at his son and would see that he was troubled; then he would stand before him and say: Poor boy, you are going about in quiet despair;* (but he never questioned him more closely; alas, he couldn't, for he too went about in a state of quiet despair). Beyond that no word was ever breathed about the matter. But within the memory of man

this father and son may have been two of the most
melancholy beings that ever lived.

That is the derivation of the term "quiet despair."
It is not used in any other context, for people generally have quite another idea of despair. Whenever
the son merely evoked the words "quiet despair" in
his mind, he would invariably break down and weep,
partly because it was so inexplicably appalling, partly
because he recalled the voice of his father who, as all
melancholy persons, was taciturn, but at the same
time, possessed the pithy weight of melancholy.

And the father thought the son's melancholy was
his fault, and the son believed the father's melancholy was his fault, and so they never spoke of it to
each other. And that exclamation which the father
made was an outbreak of his own melancholy, so
that in saying what he did he was talking to himself
rather than to his son.

33.   1850.

The most dangerous situation for a child in regard to matters of religion.

The most dangerous is not that the father or the edu-
cator is a freethinker, or even a hypocrite. No, the
most dangerous is if he is a pious, god-fearing man,
and the child is intimately and deeply sure of it, but
nevertheless senses that deep down in his father's
soul there is a hidden disquiet, as though fear of
God and piety still were powerless to give peace. The
real danger lies in the fact that on this point the
child is almost compelled to draw a conclusion about
God, namely that, after all, God is not infinitely
loving.

34.   *1844.*

A relationship between a father and a son where the son secretly discovers* everything behind the father and yet dares not know it. His father is a man whom the world esteems, god-fearing and strict; only once when he was intoxicated did he drop a few words that made the son suspect the worst. The son never had any other intimation of it, and he never dared ask his father or any one else.

35.*   *1854.*

The great benefaction of bestowing life upon another human being! Yes, most certainly! A debilitated lecher, a senile oldster, with hardly enough sexual potency—the truth is they cannot bridle their lustful heat, but this is hypocritically expressed to the effect that they intend to make the great benefaction: bestow life on another human being. Well, thank you! And what a life! A wretched, miserable, tormented existence usually becomes the lot of such progeny. Now, isn't that fine!

36.   *1848.*

Everything my father has told me comes true, yes. "There are sins from which a human being can be saved only by extraordinary divine succor." From a human viewpoint I owe my father everything. He has made me as unhappy as possible in every way, made my youth a torment without peer, caused me, inwardly, not to be far from feeling scandalized by Christianity, or, rather, I *was* scandalized, but out of reverence for it I decided never to breathe a word about it to anyone, and out of love for my father to

represent Christianity as being as true as possible in
contrast to the senseless nonsense which in Christendom passes for Christianity; and yet my father was
the most affectionate father and I always had and
always will have a deep yearning for him whom,
morning and evening, I have never once failed to
remember.

37.

✝

My father died Wednesday the 8th at 2 A.M. I had
so deeply wished him to live a few years longer, and
I regard his death as the last sacrifice he made to his
love for me, for he died not from me, but for me, in
order that perhaps something might still come of me.
Of all he left me, his memory, his transfigured image,
transfigured not through the poetic inventions of my
imagination (of that it had no need), but transfigured
through many personal touches that I only now learn
about, this memory is the most precious thing to me
and I will endeavor to keep it concealed from the
world, for I do feel that at this moment there is only
one person (E. Boesen)* with whom I can truly speak
of him. He was "a deeply faithful friend."

August 11, 1838.

38.   1838.

Then it was that the big earthquake* happened, the
terrible upheaval that suddenly obliged me to adopt
a new infallible law of interpretation of all phenomena. Then I suspected* that my father's ripe old age
was not a divine blessing, but rather a curse; that
our family's excellent mental gifts only served to ex-

cite us mutually; I felt the stillness of death rise
around me when in my father I saw a doomed man
destined to survive us all, a cross on the grave of his
own hopes. A guilt must be weighing on our entire
family; God's punishment must be upon it; our family was to vanish, swept aside by God's mighty hand,
blotted out, erased like an experiment gone wrong,
and only now and again did I find some slight relief
in the thought that on my father had been imposed
the onerous duty, by means of the comfort of religion, to soothe us all, administer the last sacrament
to us, so that, whatever happened, a better world
would be open to us, whether we lost everything here
below, or whether that punishment would strike us
which the Jews always wished over their enemies:
that all memory and trace of us would be completely
blotted out, that no one should ever find us.

39.   *1838.*

Torn to pieces as I was inside, without any prospect
of leading a humanly happy life here below ("that I
might prosper and live long in the land"),* without
any hope of a happy, cosy future—as most naturally
results from and rests in the historical continuity of
domestic family-life*—what wonder that in despair-
ing desperation I seized upon the intellectual side of
man only and clung to it so closely that the thought
of my considerable mental talents was my only consolation, ideas my only joy, human beings objects of
indifference.

40.   *1844-45.*

When Father died Sibbern* said to me: "Now you
won't ever pass your final theological examination,

will you?" But that was exactly what I did; if Father
had stayed alive I would never have made it.—When
I broke my engagement Peter* said to me: "Now
you are lost." Yet it is obvious that whatever importance, if any, I have attained, is attributable to that
step.

41.   1848.

My father's death was indeed a terribly harrowing
experience for me—*how*, I have never revealed to a
single, solitary person. Altogether the whole setting
of my early life is so cloaked in darkest melancholy
and fogs of the deepest and gloomiest brooding
wretchedness that it is no wonder I turned out as I
did. But all of this shall remain my secret.* Perhaps
on another person it would not have made such a
deep impression, but my imagination, and especially
at its awakening, before it yet had any real tasks to
turn to, was gloomy. Such primitive melancholy, such
a vast dowry of sorrow and what in the deepest sense
was tragic: being a child raised by a brooding old
man—and yet with an inborn virtuosity at being able
to deceive everybody, as though I were vivacity and
merriment incarnate—think of this, and finally that
God in Heaven has helped me as He has!

42.   *July-August, 1840.*

I am sitting here all alone (I suppose I have quite
often been just as alone, but I have not been conscious of it) counting the hours until I shall see
Saedding.* I cannot remember that my father was
ever any different, and now I am about to see the
places where, as a poor boy, he used to tend the sheep,

the places for which, because of his descriptions, I
have been homesick. Imagine if I should fall ill
now—and be buried in Saedding cemetery! Strange
thought. The last wish father expressed to me is fulfilled*—should my whole earthly destiny thereby be
fulfilled too? So be it! My task, after all, was not so
poor, seeing what I owed him. I learned from him
the meaning of fatherly love, and that gave me an
idea of the love of our heavenly Father, the only un-
shakable thing in life, the true Archimedean point.

43.   July-August 1840.

The heath must be especially influential in developing strong minds; here all lies naked, bared before
God, and here the multifarious diversions have no
place, the many odd nooks and crannies in which
our minds can hide and whence it is often hard for
serious purpose to collect the scattered thoughts.
Here the mind must close in upon itself, definitely
and exactly. "Whither shall I flee from Thy presence?"* one could ask in truth here on the heath.

44.   1846.

The awful thing about that man who once, as a small
boy tending sheep on the Jutland heath, suffering
many ills, famished and exhausted, stood up on a
hill and cursed God! And that man was never able
to forget it, not even at the age of 82.*

45.   1848.

My father died—I got another father in his stead:
God in Heaven—and then I found out that, essenti-

ally, my first father had been my stepfather and only
unessentially my first father.

46.   1848.

The best proof of the soul's immortality, that God
exists, etc., actually is the impression one received
thereof in childhood, namely the proof which, differ-
ing from the many learned and grandiloquent proofs,
could be summarized thus: It is absolutely true, because my father told me so.

2. REGINE

47.   May 8, 1837.

Oh, God, but how easily one forgets such an intention!* I have again been back in the world—dethroned* in my inner domain—in order to reign
there for some time. But oh, "for what is a man
profited if he shall gain the whole world, and lose his
own soul?" Today again (May 8), I have attempted to
forget myself, however not by means of noisy clatter;
that substitute does not help; but by going out to
Rørdam's to talk with Bolette and (if possible) by
making the devil of banter and quibbling stay behind, that spirit who with a flaming sword—as I have
deserved it—places himself between me and the heart
of every innocent maiden—when Thou overtook me,
oh Lord,* and I thank Thee for not at once letting
me lose my mind—I have never been more fearful
thereof, I thank Thee that once more Thou hast lent
me Thy ear.

48.   *May 9, 1837.*

Today again the same scene*—Still, I managed to get
to the Rørdams'—merciful God, why did this inclination have to awaken precisely at this time—Oh, how I
feel that I am alone—oh, a curse on that prideful
satisfaction at standing alone—All will despise me
now—Oh, but Thou, my God, I pray Thee, abandon
me not—suffer me to live and become a better man.

49.   *1837.*

Like a lone spruce fir, egotistically circumscribed,
pointing toward loftier spheres, I stand, casting no
shadow, and only the stock-dove builds its nest in my
branches.   Sunday, July 9, in Frederiksberg Park
                 after calling on the Rørdams.

50.

Thou queen of my heart (*"Regina"*),* enfolded in
the deepest recesses of my heart, in the most vital
fullness of my thought, equidistant from Heaven and
Hell—unknown Divinity! Oh, can I really believe
what the poets sing: that when a man sees his beloved
for the first time he believes that he has seen her
long before, that all love, as all understanding, is
memory, that love, also in the individual, has its
prophecies, its types, its myths, its Old Testament.
Everywhere, in every girl's face, I see features re-
minding me of your beauty, but it seems to me I
would need all the girls in the world to distil, as it
were, your beauty from theirs, that I would have to
circumnavigate the world to find the continent I
miss, yet which the deepest secret of my whole being

polarically* indicates;—and the next instant you are
so close to me, so present, so powerfully investing my
spirit that I feel myself to be transfigured, and feel
it is good to be here.

Oh, blind god of Love! You who see into our hidden recesses, will you reveal love to me? Shall I find
here below what I seek, shall I experience the *Conclusion* drawn from all my life's eccentric premises,*
am I to hold you in my arms—or *do you order me to
be on my way?**

Have you gone before me, my *yearning*, are you
beckoning to me, transfigured, from another world?
Oh, I will cast off everything to become light enough
to follow you.

February 2, 1839.

51.   1849.

In the summer of '40 I passed my final theological
examination.

Then, without further ado, I called at her house.*
I went to Jutland, and maybe baited the hook for her
a little already then (for instance, by lending them
books* in my absence and in one of them causing
them to read a special passage).

I returned in August. The period from August 9
until September, strictly speaking can be said to be
the period in which I made my approaches to her.

On September 8, I left home with the firm intention of getting the whole thing settled. We met in
the street just outside their house. She said that no
one was at home. I was foolhardy enough to interpret
this as an invitation, as just what I needed. I went
up with her. There we stood, the two of us alone in

the living room. She was a little flustered. I asked
her to play something for me as was her wont. She
does it, but I cannot make a successful opening. Then
I suddenly seize the music sheet, close it, not without
a certain impetuosity, throw it along the piano and
say: What do I care for music, it is you I seek; I have
sought you for 2 years. She remained silent. Actually
I have done nothing to captivate her; I have even
warned her against myself, against my melancholy.
And when she mentioned a certain relationship with
Schlegel I said: then let that relationship be a paren-
thesis, for after all I hold the priority. (NB. On second thought it was probably not until the 10th she
mentioned Schlegel,* for on the 8th she did not say
a word.) She remained essentially silent. I finally left,
for I really feared that some one might come and
find us together and notice that she was rather disturbed. I went directly to the State Councilor. I knew
that I was terribly afraid of having made too strong
an impression on her, and also that my visit somehow
might cause some misunderstanding, maybe even be
damaging to her reputation.

Her father said neither Yes nor No; still he was
willing enough as I easily gathered. I asked for an
appointment and received it for the afternoon of
September 10. I have not uttered a single word to
beguile her—her answer was yes.

Instantly I initiated relations with the entire family. My virtuosity was called into play, particularly
vis à vis her father whom, by the way, I have always
liked very much indeed.

But inwardly . . . ! the second day I saw that I had
made a mistake. A person like myself, doing pen-

ance,* my *vita ante acta,* my melancholy . . . that was all it took.

I suffered indescribably during that time.

She appeared not to notice anything. On the contrary, toward the end she got so much above herself that she declared she had accepted me from pity, in brief, I hardly ever saw such overweening pride.

This, in a sense, became the dangerous part. If she does not take it more to heart, I thought, than, as she herself once said: "If I believed it was from habit you came I would instantly break it off"—as I say, if she does not take it more to heart, then I am well off. In another sense—I admit my weakness—for a moment she made me angry.

Now I put forces to work—she truly gives in, and the exact opposite follows, the most extreme giving herself over (from adoration, something for which I was responsible to a certain extent, because I myself, comprehending only too clearly the difficulty of the relationship and realizing that the greatest force had to be applied to compel my melancholy to get the upper hand, if possible, had said to her: give yourself; by showing pride you make the matter [of breaking off] easy. A completely true remark, sincere toward her, and darkly treacherous toward myself).

Naturally now my melancholy is reawakened, for her giving herself means that I am again "responsible" in the highest possible measure—whereas her "pride" to a certain extent relieved me of "responsibility"—I see that a break must come. My judgment is, and my idea was, that it is God's chastisement of me.

I cannot quite make out what impression she has

made on me in a purely erotic sense. For it is certain
that the fact that she had given herself almost in
adoration, and asked me to love her, moved me so
strongly that I would risk everything for her. Still,
how highly I loved her is also evidenced thereby that
I constantly have wanted to conceal to myself how
much she really moved me, but this, after all, has no
essential relation to the Erotic.

If I had not been a penitent, not had my *vita ante
acta,* not been melancholy, then the bond with her
would have made me as happy as I could never hitherto have dreamed of becoming. But even though I
had to say—because unfortunately I am the person I
am—that I could become happier in unhappiness
without her than *with* her—still she had moved me
and I would willingly, nay, more than willingly, have
done everything.

Yet she has had some inkling of how it was with
me. For quite frequently this remark occurred: You
will never be happy anyway, so it can't really matter
one way or the other whether I am allowed to stay
with you. Once she also said that she would never
question me about anything, if only she might stay
with me.

But as I understood it, there was a divine protest
against our union. The marriage ceremony. I would
have to keep silent about a very great deal, base it
all on an untruth.

I wrote to her, returning her ring. The note is
reproduced textually in *"The Psychological Experiment."* * I have deliberately left it purely historical,
for I have never spoken to anyone about it, not
to a single solitary person. I am more silent than a

tomb. If she should happen to see the book I just intended to remind her of it.

During those two months of deceit I observed the prudent measure of telling her, at intervals, straight out: Give in, let me go; you will not be able to stand it. To which she replied passionately that she would rather stand anything than let me go.

I also suggested giving the matter another appearance, namely that it was she who broke with me—in order to spare her all mortification. She did not want that; she answered that if she could bear the rest, she probably could bear that too, and she added, not unsocratically,* that no one, she presumed, would make her feel it in her presence, and what they said about her when she was absent could make no difference.

The break came—about two months later. She was in despair. For the first time in my life I chided her. It was the only thing to do.

Leaving her, I went directly to the theater because I wanted to meet Emil Boesen. (At the time a story was fabricated that made the rounds of the city, namely that I was supposed to have told the family, taking out my watch, that if they had any more to say, please hurry, for I was going to the theater.) The act was over. As I was leaving my seat in the back rows of the orchestra, the State Councilor comes toward me from the front rows and says: May I talk to you? We went to his house. She is in despair, he said. It will be the death of her, she is in deep despair. I said: I will calm her down, but the matter is settled. He said: I am a proud man; it is hard, but I beg of you, do not break with her. He was truly great; I was quite shaken. But I held on to my own view. I had supper with the family. Spoke with her as I was leaving. The next morning I received a letter from him saying that she had not slept all night, that I must come and see her. I went, and made her see reason. She asked: Will you never marry? I replied: Yes, in ten years when I shall have sown all my wild oats, I shall need a young-blooded miss to rejuvenate me.—A necessary cruelty. Then she said: Forgive me for what I have done to you. I replied: I am the one to ask *your* forgiveness. She said: Promise me that you will think of me. I did. She said: Kiss me. I did —but without passion. Merciful God!

To step out of the relationship as a cad, perhaps as an arch-cad, was the only thing to do; to put her on an even keel and start her on her course toward another marriage; but at the same time it was exquisite chivalry. With my nimble brain it certainly had been quite easy for me to withdraw on cheaper conditions.—

That such behavior is chivalrous has been developed by the young man in Constantin Constantius* and I agree with him.

Thereupon our ways parted. I spent the nights weeping on my bed. But during the day I was the usual personage, more flippant and full of banter than was really called for. My brother said to me that he would go to the family and prove to them that I was no cad. I said: If you do that I'll put a bullet through your head.—The best proof of how deeply concerned I was about the matter.

I went to Berlin. I suffered very, very much. I

thought of her every day. Until now I have kept up without fail: to pray for her every day at least once, often twice, besides thinking about her in other ways.

When the bond broke my feeling was this: either you plunge into wild dissipation—or absolute religiousness, but of another brand than the parson's "melange."*

"*A Seducer's Diary*" was written for her sake, to help push her boat from ashore.* The foreword to the *Two Edifying Discourses* is intended for her, as much else; the book's date* and dedication are for my father. In the book there are tenuous hints about giving up, to the effect that one only loses the beloved by making him act against his conviction. She has read it; I know it through Sibbern.

52.   1848.

Remark: "Oh, how hard to be as old as eternity makes one, when one is still a man, mostly a man, and when the whole of existence talks to one in the language of youth. There was a young girl I loved; she was lovely, and so young (how blissful it must be to be young like that!) and persuasive and inciting. Oh, terrible grief: I was an eternity too old for her."

53.   1848.

The greatest possible misunderstanding about religious matters between one human being and another occurs when you take a man and a woman, and the man wants to teach her religion, and the whole bliss inherent therein, in this being *for* God, then becomes the object of her amorous love.

54.   *1848.*

Quite strange! In one of my first talks with her when
I was most deeply shaken and had been stirred to the
depths of my being, I told her: that in each generation there are a few persons destined to be sacrificed
for the rest. Most likely she did not understand what
I was talking about, perhaps I didn't make myself
clear (in any case only about my inward suffering,
really) least of all did I understand that it would start
making her suffer. But precisely her spontaneous,
young happiness in juxtaposition to my horrible
melancholy, and in such a relationship as ours, compelled me to try to understand myself; for I had
never before suspected the extent of my melancholy;
I had had no true yardstick for measuring how happy
a human being could be.

Thus I believed myself sacrificed, because I understood that my suffering and anguish made me inven-
tive in delving for the Truth which, in turn, might
benefit others.

Since then God has guided me ever forward, and
now I stand at the point where, externally too, it
becomes true, that there are some people who are
sacrificed for the rest.

55.   *1848.*

There exists a prophetic saying by her about me:
Surely you will end up a Jesuit. For to a youthful,
romantic imagination Jesuitism* represents a striving, the τελος [aim]* of which is completely beyond
the grasp of such youthfulness.

56.   *October 25, 1841.*

. . . You say, "what I have lost, or rather deprived
myself of"; alas, how could you know or understand
what I have lost. On this matter you had better keep
silent—and how should anyone know better than I,
who have made my whole extremely meditative soul
into a setting, as tasteful as possible, for her pure and
deep, and my dark, thoughts, my melancholy dreams,
my brilliant hopes—and above all, this my ever
changeable instability, in brief, all my brilliancy as
opposed to her depth—and then when I grew dizzy
as I gazed down into her infinite affection—for nothing, after all, is as infinite as love—or when her emotions were not so profound, but danced over the deep
in the light play of love—what I have lost: the only
thing I loved; what I have lost: in the eyes of the
world my word as a gentleman, in which I always
have placed and will place my honor, my joy, my
pride—namely to be faithful. . . . Yet my soul is as
disturbed as my body in the moment I am writing
this, in a cabin rocked by the twofold movements of
a steamer.

And it is hard for me, precisely in the present case,
where I so strongly desired to act, to see myself relegated to an activity otherwise left to women and
children—viz. to pray.

You say: She was beautiful. Oh, what do you know
about that; I know it, for this beauty cost me tears—I
bought flowers to adorn her; I would have decked
her out with all the embellishments in the world—of
course only in the measure that they would have
served to set off her grace—and then, when she was
there, attired in all her finery, I had to leave—when

her soul-joyous, life-loving gaze met mine, then I had to leave—then I "went out and wept bitterly."*

She did not love my shapely nose, nor my fine eyes, nor my small feet, nor my smart brain—she loved only me, and yet she did not understand me.—

3. POUL MØLLER

April.   57.   *1838.*

Again a long period has elapsed in which I have been unable to pull myself together for the least little thing —I shall now try to get going again.

Poul Møller is dead.*

58.   *1838.*

I wanted to hear Nielsen* recite: "Rejoicing about Denmark," but I felt so strangely moved by the words:

"Do you remember the widely-traveled man?"
Yes, indeed, now he has traveled far—but I, for one, shall certainly remember him.

April 2.

59.

The Extraordinary

I remember a remark by Poul Møller as he lay dying, which he used to make to me quite frequently while he was still among the living and which, if I am not mistaken (besides the remark: tell little K. he must see to it not to lay out too extensive a plan of studies, as that has harmed me greatly) he enjoined Sibbern to repeat to me again and again: You are so thoroughly "polemicized" that it is quite awful.

Whether on his deathbed P.M. told Sibbern to make that remark to me (You are so thoroughly polemicized, etc.) I can not remember for sure, but I am almost inclined to doubt it. However, as to the other remark, I recall very well that he enjoined Sibbern to tell me when S. talked with P.M. the last time before P.M. died. And as to the first remark (you are so thoroughly polemicized) it was an expression he constantly used to me while he was alive, and S. has taken it up after him and used it against me several times.

III

KIERKEGAARD AS A WRITER

60.   *1847.*
Something about my Punctuation

In regard to spelling I bow unconditionally to Authority (Molbech):* it never occurs to me to investigate further, for I know that on this point I lack knowledge, wherefore I willingly admit that I believe every fair-to-middling Danish author is perhaps more diligent in this respect than I.

Punctuation is something else again; in that I do not bow unconditionally to anyone, and I greatly doubt whether there is any Danish author who can match me in that respect. My whole structure as a dialectician* with an unusual sense of the rhetorical, my constant intercourse with my thoughts by silent conversations, my experience in reading aloud: all these must needs make me excel in this respect.

That is why I make distinctions in my punctuation. In a scientific paper I use my punctuation differently from the way I use it in rhetorical writing. This probably already will be quite enough for most people, who only acknowledge one grammar. It goes without saying that in regard to punctuation I

certainly would not dare to proffer my writings as
direct examples for schoolboys or quite young people. Similarly, a good Latin teacher usually does not
teach his students the finer shades of that language,
such as the delightful little mysteries of the conjunc-
tive mood, but he himself will use them. Unfortunately I do not really know any Danish author who,
in an ideal sense, pays proper attention to punctuation; they merely follow the grammatical norm. My
punctuation deviates especially in rhetorical matters,
because there it becomes more evolved. What particularly occupies me is the architectonic-dialectical
phenomenon that the eye sees the structure of the
sentences which at the same time, when one reads
them aloud, becomes their rhythm—and in my mind's
eye I always visualize a reader reading aloud.—That
again is the reason why I sometimes use commas very
sparingly. For instance, where I want a subdivision
under a semicolon, I do not place a comma between
such sentences. I write, for example, "what one owes
to another or what one owes to one's self." In this
respect I keep up a constant feud with compositors
who, with the best intentions, put commas everywhere and by so doing disturb my rhythm.

In my opinion most Danish stylists use the period
sign entirely erroneously. They cut up their discourse
in nothing but short periods with the result that logic
is deprived of the respect it should command, that
sentences which logically are dependent instead become co-ordinated by each forming a period.

Above all I must repeat that I imagine to myself
readers reading aloud and therefore well versed in

following the vibration of every thought into its last recess, and also are able to recreate this with the voice. I am willing to submit, with complete confidence, to the test that an actor or an orator used to modulating should read, as an experiment, a small fragment of my discourses: and I am convinced that he will admit that *much* of what ordinarily he must determine for himself, *much* that otherwise is elucidated by instructive hints on the part of the author, in my text he will find to be indicated by punctuation. Abstract, grammatical punctuation in no wise suffices when it comes to the Rhetorical, particularly if this is spiced with a dash of the Ironical, the Epigrammatic, the Subtle, and what, in the sense of the idea, would be the Malicious, etc.

61.   *1843.*

Quite curious, I must say. I had decided to change the small foreword* to the "Two Sermons," because I somehow felt that it concealed a certain spiritual eroticism, and because it is so extraordinarily hard for me to give myself so calmly that the polemic contrast is not pointedly present. So I rush to the printing shop. What happens? The compositor intercedes for this foreword. Though I laughed a little at him I thought to myself: "So let him be 'the individual reader,' my reader." In my joy about this idea I first decided to have only 2 copies printed and present one of them to the compositor. There was really something fine in seeing his emotion. A compositor who, one would think, gets even more bored with a manuscript than the author himself!

62.   *1847.*

For many years my melancholy has had the effect of preventing me from saying "Thou" to myself, from being on intimate terms with myself in the deepest sense. Between my melancholy and my intimate "Thou" there lay a whole world of phantasy. This world it is that I have partly exhausted in my pseudonyms.* Just like a person who hasn't a happy home spends as much time away from it as possible and would prefer to be rid of it, so my melancholy has kept me away from my own self while I, making discoveries and poetical experiences, traveled through a world of phantasy. Like a person who has taken over a big estate cannot get through finding out all about it, so, because of my melancholy, was my relation to opportunity.

63.   November 5, 1846.

Perhaps—I won't say more, for I well know how difficult it is to judge *in abstracto* about one's own self if he wants to judge correctly—I might now have succeeded in interrupting my creative work and concentrate on taking up some official position if everything had been as it should be and it was clear that it was freedom which turned the scales. Now it is not possible. For me to become a minister would present a great difficulty; if I took it upon myself I might risk becoming a stumbling-block as formerly in connection with my engagement. For another thing, living in the country in complete seclusion would now be difficult for me because I actually am somewhat embittered so that I need the enchantment of creative work to help me forget life's mean pettinesses.

I realize more and more that I am so constituted that I shall not succeed in realizing my ideals, while in another sense, and precisely in the human sense, I shall grow far beyond my ideals. Ordinarily, most people aim their ideals at the Great, the Extraordinary, which they never attain. I am far too melancholy to harbor such ideals. Others would smile at my ideals. It is certainly true that my ideal was simply to become a husband, to live solely for being married. And lo and behold, while I despair of attaining that goal I become an author and, who knows, maybe a ranking author. My next ideal was to become a minister in a rural parish and live amid quiet scenery, become an integral part of the small circle surrounding me—and lo and behold, as I despair of attaining that, it is quite possible that I shall again realize something that will appear much greater.

When Bishop Mynster* advises me to become a village pastor he evidently does not understand me. It is certainly true that it is my wish, but our premises are entirely different. He assumes that, in some way or other, I wish to make a career of it, that I aspire to become somebody, but there, precisely, is the rub: I aspire to be as little as possible; that is precisely the core of my melancholy. For that very reason I have been content to be regarded as half-mad, though this merely was a negative form of being something out of the ordinary. And this may quite possibly remain my essential form of existence, and I shall never attain the pleasant, becalmed existence of being something very small.

What I have always known within myself, and the reason why I never have spoken to a soul about my real concerns, I have again found to be true after talking with Bishop Mynster: it leads nowhere, for as I cannot and dare not talk about that which totally and essentially constitutes my innermost existence,* the conversation almost becomes a deceit on my part. In relation to a man like Mynster—because I revere him so highly—I feel ever more deeply how woeful that is.

64.   *1847.*

Only when I write do I feel well. Then I forget all of life's vexations, all its sufferings, then I am wrapped in thought and am happy. If I stop for a few days, right away I become ill, overwhelmed and troubled; my head feels heavy and burdened. So powerful an urge, so ample, so inexhaustible, one which, having subsisted day after day for five or six years, is still flowing as richly as ever, such an urge, one would think, must also be a vocation from God. If these great riches of thought, still latent in my soul, must be repressed, it will be anguish and torture for me, and I shall become an absolute good-for-nothing. And why should they be repressed? Because I have the idea of torturing myself, of doing penance, through forcing myself into something for which verily, if I understand myself right, I am ultimately unfitted. No, God forbid! Nor does God, I presume, want to remain without testimony in external matters either. It is hard and depressing to exhaust one's capital in order to be allowed to work more industriously and more strenuously than any man in the kingdom of Denmark. It is hard and depressing that as a result of all this toil one becomes the butt of the craven jealousy of the aristocracy and of the mockery of the populace! It is hard and depressing that the outlook is this: If I work still harder things will become still worse! But of course I will gladly and patiently put up with all this if only I could win true inward security, and that it would not be my duty to force myself into self-chosen martyrdom by taking up a position which in a certain sense of course I might desire, but which, nonetheless, I could neither fill properly nor really be happy in. Being an author, on the contrary, is not self-chosen; it is concomitant with everything in my individuality and its deepest urge.

May God then give me good fortune and succor and above all a certain spirit, yes, a certain spirit to resist the onslaughts of doubt and temptation that rise within me, for after all it is not too hard to do battle with the world.

The same thing will happen with me as at the time of my engagement. Only, God be praised, the difference this time is that I am not wronging another human being, I am not breaking any given pledge; but the similarity is that I must again sail the high seas, live willy-nilly, surrendering myself unconditionally to God's will. Of course it is more secure to have a solid position in life, some official appointment which does not demand nearly as much of one —but in God's name, the other thing, by God, is still more secure. But it takes faith; you need faith at every turn, every instant. That is the difference. Most people lead far too sheltered lives, and for that reason they get to know God so little. They have permanent positions, they never put in their utmost effort; they have tranquillity with wife and children—and I, for one, shall never talk deprecatingly about that happiness—but I believe it is my task to do without all this. Why in the world should that which we read* in the New Testament again and again not be permitted? But the unfortunate thing is that people have no idea at all of what it means to be a Christian, and that is why I am left without sympathy, that is why I am not understood.

65.   1847.

I never have had any intimate confidant. As a writer I have, in a way, used the public as my confidant. But in regard to my relations with the public I must again make posterity my confidant. After all, the same people who are supposed to come and laugh at one, cannot very well be used as confidants.

66.   1847.

If I had not had independent means I would have been on a good footing with our contemporary age. First of all, I would not have been able to spare the time for writing the big sequels of my work; my performance would have been like everyone else's. Then one is loved. It would have been nothing but trivia—then one is read.

Literary criticism is non-existent in Denmark. The recipe for reviews in the daily papers is like this: If I have written fifty-three sheets the review at most will be one column, but if I write a 10-page pamphlet the review will fill a whole issue, maybe two. And this effrontery is much appreciated in a small town, for of course there are at most only two or three authors who suffer thereby; all the scribblers derive plenty

of benefit by a big work being treated as a trifle and
a pamphlet as something very important.

67.   June 9, 1847.

Here, in a sense, is the rub of all my misfortune; if
I had not had any private means I should never have
been able to safeguard the awful secret of my melancholy. (Merciful God, what a horrible wrong my
father did me with his melancholy—an old man un-
burdening all his gloom on a wretched child, not to
mention the even more terrible thing, and yet, with
it all, the best of fathers.) On the other hand, if he
had not done this to me I would not have become the
person I am today. I would have been *constrained*
to become insane, or else to have forged my way to
the top. As it is, I have succeeded in turning a somer-
sault into the realm of pure spirit where I now live.
But that, in turn, made me absolutely heterogenous
with ordinary humanity. What essentially I lack is
a body and physical presuppositions.

68.   1847.

What our contemporary age really needs is education. With that in view God picked a man who also
needed education and raised him *privatissime* so that
he, in turn, could teach to others what he himself
had learned.

69.

How I understood my whole activity as a writer.
1846.

I am, in the deepest sense, an unhappy individual
who since my earliest days have been nailed fast to
some suffering* close to insanity, the deeper cause of

which must have its roots in some disproportion between my soul and my body; for (and this is both a strange thing and also my infinite encouragement) it has no relation to my mind and spirit which, on the contrary, and perhaps because of the tense relationship between my soul and my body, have acquired a tensile strength rarely seen.

An old man who himself was extremely melancholy (in what way I shall not record) begets a son in his old age who inherits all this melancholy, but at the same time has a resourceful mind that enables him to conceal it; and because his spirit essentially and in an eminent sense is sound, his melancholy cannot get the better of him, but neither is he capable of mastering it; at most, his spirit enables him to *bear* it.

A young girl (who in painfully overweening pride reveals vast strength and thus dimly lets me perceive a loophole through which to escape from what had been started by a tragic misunderstanding, breaking off an engagement, for she let me suspect a strength in her, as if she did not care one way or the other) at the most solemn moment places a murder on my conscience; a troubled father solemnly assures me that it will indeed mean the girl's death.* Whether she was trifling is no concern of mine.

From that moment I dedicated my life to serving an idea according to my small capacity, but with maximum effort.

Though not a friend of others being privy to my secrets, though definitely disinclined to speak to others about my innermost being, I still hold the opinion, and always have, that it is a man's duty not to neglect the court of appeal that is offered him by taking counsel with another human being; only this must not deteriorate into flippant intimacy, but must be earnest, responsible communication. I therefore spoke to my doctor to find out whether he thought that this imbalance in my frame between the physical and psychic could be overcome so that I could "realize the universal" [lead an ordinary life]. He doubted it. I asked him whether he thought that the mind —through will-power—was capable of transforming or reshaping such basic malformation; he doubted it; he would not even advise me to harness all my will-power (of which he has an idea), as it might result in my exploding the whole thing.

From that instant my choice was made. That grievous malformation with its attendant sufferings (which undoubtedly would have caused most others to commit suicide, if they had had enough spirit left to grasp the utter misery of that torture) is what I have regarded as the thorn* in the flesh, my limitation, my cross; and I have believed that this was the high purchase price which God in Heaven demanded of me in exchange for a strength of mind and spirit that seeks its equal among my contemporaries. This does not make me boastful, *for I am crushed anyhow*, and my wish has become a daily bitter pain and humiliation to me.

Without daring to plead any revelations or things of that nature, I have conceived of myself as intent upon standing up for the Ordinary—in a bungled and demoralized age—and making it lovable and accessible to all those of my fellow-creatures who are capable of realizing it, but who are led astray by the times and who chase* after the Un-Common, the

Extra-Ordinary. I have understood my task to be like
that of a person who himself has become unhappy
and therefore—if he loves human beings—particularly
desires to help others who are capable of realizing
happiness.

But since my task also implied a pious attempt, in
all humility to do something good to make up for my
shortcomings, I have been especially vigilant that my
efforts should not be tainted with self-seeking vanity
and, above all, that I served Thought and Truth in
such a way as not to derive any secular and temporal
advantages therefrom. Therefore I know, in all good
conscience, that I have worked with true resignation.

As my work progressed I constantly thought that I
was gaining a better understanding of God's will with
me: that I bear the anguish whereby God has put his
reins on me, and then perhaps perform the Extra-
Ordinary.

If I should give a closer description of my conception of all the details of my life this journal would
grow into a voluminous folio which only a very few
would be knowledgeable and earnest enough to understand. Nor do I have time for writing down anything like that.

I can truly say that I have my strength in frailty
and weakness.* It never would occur to me, for example, that a girl would refuse me, if I were inwardly
sure that I dared do everything to win her; it never
would occur to me that I would not be able to accomplish the most astonishing things if only I were inwardly sure that I dared tackle them. In the latter
lies my wretchedness, in the former my almost super-
natural feeling of strength. Most people are in the

contrary situation: they fear resistance from the out-side, and do not know the horrible pain of inward resistance. I, on the other hand, have no fear what-ever of external resistance, but there is an inner resistance when God lets me feel the thorn that ran-kles—that is my visitation.

70. *1848.*

Oh, how terrifying it is when thus for a moment I come to think of my life's dark background from the very earliest moment. The anguished fear my father put into my soul, his own terrible melancholy, the many things on that account which I cannot even note down. I conceived a great fear of Christianity, and yet I felt strongly drawn to it. And then later on, what did I not suffer on account of Peter* when he fell into the morbid grip of religion.

As I said, it is terrible to think even for a moment of the life I thus have led in the most hidden recesses of my soul, of course literally without ever having breathed a word about it to a single person, not even daring to set down the slightest hint about it—and then to think that I have been able to disguise this life under the cloak of an outward existence of exu-berance and gaiety.

How true, therefore, is the remark I have often made about myself that like Sheherazade* who saved her life by telling fairy tales, so I save my life or keep myself alive by writing.

71. *1847.*

Now, Andersen [Hans Christian] can tell the tale about "The Galoshes of Fortune"—but I can tell the tale of the shoe that pinches, or rather I could tell it, but precisely because I choose not to tell it, but to bury it in deep silence, I am able to tell a good deal of other things.

72.   1846.

I wanted particularly to represent the various stages* of life, if possible in one work, and that is how I consider all my pseudonymous writings. With that in mind it was important to keep an unvarying balance so that, for instance, the Religious should not appear at a later time when I had become so much older that my style would have lost some of the lofty, imaginative expansiveness proper to the Esthetic. The idea is not that Religious should have this exuberance, but that the writer should be capable of producing it and making it clear that if the Religious lacked this style the reason certainly was not that the writer lacked the necessary youthfulness.

Supposing some other author might have been capable of performing the same work; yet, if he had not finished it within 5 or 6 years he would never be able to do it. Thus, my whole undertaking stands rather isolated, not only in and by itself, but good fortune attended it too.

There was another reason why I had to speed up this work, though by observing the strictest discipline I prevented myself from omitting even the smallest comma: the state of my finances does not permit me to continue for long to serve, to the same extent as heretofore, the idea of combined judge and midwife (the judging-maieutic* idea). It has not been "judging"* in the direct sense of denouncing loudly—but, indirectly, by acting and coining epigrams on our times.

However, I have actually erected a stumbling-block against myself through my consistency. Had I been only half so consistent I should already at this moment be much better understood. But the Lord takes greater delight in obedience* than in the fat of the ram ["to hearken is better than the fat of rams" Samuel I, 15, 22]. And consistency is dearer to thought than worldly recognition from society gossips.

I am supposed to be slipshod, believe it or not. I am fully convinced that no other Danish author gives to the slightest word so extreme an attention as I do. Two rewrites* by my own hand of everything; three or four rewrites of large parts; add to that (of which no one has the least idea) my meditations during my strolls, and the fact that I have recited everything to myself many times before writing it down—and that they call "being slipshod"! And why? Because people have no idea of the work it takes, an author being a person who sits in his room and writes for certain hours of the day, and for the rest of the time leaves his ideas alone. Such an author, when he resumes work, spends time on getting going again, whereas I come home with everything fully thought out, and even knowing it by heart in its stylistic form.

So almost always when people read a couple of pages by me they are amazed at my style—but a big book—oh, how would that be possible—*ergo*: it must be slipshod dabbling, whereas the truth is that if a man wills One thing with his every effort and sacrifice, then it is possible.

In a way I feel a loathing for existence—for I who

love only one idea, namely that a man can become
what he really *wills*—I stand as an epigram* on human beings, their judgment of me being that they
simply cannot comprehend my consistency,* a sad
evidence of the categories, of the mediocrity, in which
they have their being.

73.

Something on Style   *1854.*

How childish it is to be deceived by such things—alas,
how true were Socrates's words: "It seems to me that
now that I am 70 years old I should no longer polish
up my style like a boy"—and though it very rarely
occurs to me now to do so, still, suddenly my old urge
may be aroused, a little sadly, to take delight in the
linguistic form. You see, I believe that as a prose-
writer I am able to achieve, merely through linguistic
form, beautiful and true effects not to be surpassed
by a poet.

As an example let me take an idea (and it is precisely this example that forced itself upon my attention today and pleaded its cause so eloquently that
it actually has made me seize my pen for the sake of
such childishness); an idea, I say, inherently rather
succinct: Everything disappoints—hope or the hoped
for. (*Marginal note*: The phrase: "Hope disappoints
or the hoped for" is by Schopenhauer.) Already there
is form, as the dash represents form. But perhaps the
idea is too summarily expressed. The idea may also
be expressed by a somewhat longer phrase and then a
linguistic twining: Everything disappoints: Hope, the
hoped for does not come, or the hoped for comes—
and disappoints. (*Marginal note*: The sentence, viz.

that hope disappoints is quite an ordinary remark; what must be stressed is the second sentence. Therefore, if I imagined a person who passionately had experienced that 'the hoped for disappoints' this special linguistic form will attract him or satisfy him. On hearing the first part [Hope disappoints] he will become impatient and think: must we hear this nonsense again now, but then the formulation of the next sentence will satisfy him completely.)

Thus I have sometimes been able to sit for hours in love with the way a language sounds, that is, if the conciseness of an idea is echoed in it; thus I could sit for hours on end, alas, like a flutist entertaining himself on his flute. Most of what I write has been spoken aloud over and over, sometimes maybe scores of times, has been heard before it was written down. (*Marginal note*: In another sense most of what I write is written down *currente calamo*,* as the saying goes, but that is because I give the final polish to my work while I am walking.) As far as I am concerned my construction of periods might be called a world of memories, for I have lived through, enjoyed, and experienced so much in this coming into being of ideas and their quest until they found their right form of expression, if, in a certain sense, it was not inherent in them at the first instant, then until even the smallest detail was adapted to it, so that the idea, as the saying goes, could feel that its form was a perfect fit (for this stylistic detail-work came later—anyone who has ideas has them in a spontaneous form).

—and then the Danish reading public! Oh how true what happened, so true to form, so characteristic! For the most part my contemporaries have been

busily occupied with my manner of dress which, of
all that concerned me, they have understood best.
About these my contemporaries in regard to me one
might say: they chose the better part. I do not com-
plain; in a certain sense I owe very, very much to the
bestiality of the times; besides I believe it would have
been the same for me in any other age.

74.   *1849.*

If I had not been strictly raised in the Christian religion, had not had all that inner suffering from early
childhood, intensified precisely at the moment when
I definitively started my career: if I hadn't had that,
and still had known what I know now, then I would
have become a poet and would actually have become
that interesting poet χατ'εξοχην* [in an eminent sense].
There has hardly lived any poet before me with a
deeper knowledge of existence and especially of the
Religious.

But it is at this point that I deviate, and the position is the old one from *Either-Or*: I will not be a
poet as *A* says, in one sense, and as *B* agrees to* in a
much deeper sense, indeed declares to be the only
one of *A*'s many ideas he completely approves of.

What does it mean to be a poet? It means to have
one's own personal life, one's reality in categories
quite different from those of poetic creation; it is to
be related to an idea in imagination only so that one's
own personal existence is more or less a satire on the
poetical and on oneself. To that extent all ranking
modern thinkers are also poets (I mean the German
ones, for surely there are no Danish ones at all). Altogether, that is the maximum of what life shows.

Most people live entirely devoid of ideas; then there are the very few who relate themselves poetically to the ideal, but refute it in their personal lives. In that way parsons are poets, and being parsons they are, in a much deeper sense than poets, "deceivers," as Socrates already called the poets.

However, as everywhere else demoralization has also set in here and Place No. 1 has been eliminated, while Place No. 2 has become No. 1. No evidence of anyone maintaining a relation to the ideal in his personal life is ever seen. That kind of life is only for the "Witness of Truth."* This rubric has ceased to exist long ago, and priests, professors of philosophy and poets now occupy the position as servants of the Truth—which I imagine is quite advantageous to them—though less so to Truth.

IV

THE CORSAIR

1. CONTEMPORARY LITERATURE

75.   *1843.*

Really, an author's lot has gradually deteriorated to
be the most wretched state of all. An author ordinarily must present himself like the gardener's help in
the vignette in *Adresseavisen* [a Copenhagen paper],
hat in hand, bowing and cringing, recommending
himself with fine letters of introduction. How stupid:
one who writes must understand that about which
he writes better than he who reads; otherwise he
would not write.

Or one must manage to become a shrewd little
pocket-lawyer proficient at gulling the public.—That
I will not do, no I won't; no I won't—no, the Devil
take the whole caboodle. I write the way I want to,
and that's the way it's going to be; the rest can do
what they like, they can stop buying, stop reading,
stop reviewing, etc.

76.   *1844.*

In our day and age book-writing has become so poor,
and people write about matters which they have never

given any real thought, let alone, experienced. I therefore have decided to read only the writings of men who have been executed or have risked their lives in some way.

77.   *1846.*

Everyone today can write a fairly decent article about all and everything; but no one can or will bear the strenuous work of following through a single solitary thought into its most tenuous logical ramifications. Instead, writing trivia is particularly appreciated today, and whoever writes a big book almost invites ridicule. In former days people read big books, and if they did read pamphlets or periodicals they did not quite like to admit it. Now everyone feels in duty bound to read what is printed in a periodical or a pamphlet, but is ashamed to have read a big book through to the end, as he fears he may be considered weak in the head.

78.   *1844 (?).*

I beg to be spared any and every critical review, for I loathe a literary critic as much as an ambulant barber-journeyman who runs after me with his shaving-bowl, which he uses for the beards of all his clients, and then dabs my face all over with his wet fingers.

79.   *1846.*

In Danish literature today the fees even for authors of repute are very small, whereas the tips being dropped in the hats of literary hacks are very considerable. The more contemptible a man of letters is today, the more money he earns.

80.   *1846.*

In regard to matters of literature and reviewing the
Berlingske Tidende may best be compared to sand-
wich paper (in regard to its principal job: political
matters, that is something else again); one reads it
while he is eating, and for lack of a napkin I have
even seen a man wipe his hands on the newspaper.
But it is true of everything that the surroundings
are of great importance, so if one wants to offer something to make a reader, if possible, a little serious,
although the material is not so high that it cannot
very well be understood by everyone, then that is
not the way to do it. That is why I never wished to
see anything of mine printed in the *Berlingske Tidende*. In preference to the circulation my works
might obtain by being printed in the *B.T.* I would
much rather have only ONE reader.

81.

"Peddlers-of-Opinion: Journalists"*
        (*A. Schopenhauer*)   *1854.*

This expression by Schopenhauer is really valuable,
and he himself realized its value. (*Marginal note*: In
one respect it is almost unpleasant for me that I have
happened to read Schopenhauer. I feel such indescribable scruples about eventually using expressions
etc. by another writer without calling due attention
to it. But his way of expressing himself is sometimes
so closely related to my own that perhaps, from exaggerated punctiliousness, I end up by ascribing to him

what is actually my own.) He points out that while in external matters most people would be ashamed of such things as wearing a hat, coat, etc. handed down from another person, this does not at all apply to matters of the mind. There practically everyone is wearing hand-me-downs. Of course the mass of human beings have no opinions, but—look out—! this drawback is being remedied by the journalists who earn their living by peddling opinions. Of course, as he properly adds, what people get is on the same order as the togs carnival-stores generally rent out.

The thing is quite natural, though. As more and more persons are torn out of the innocent state of not being obliged to have any opinion at all, and driven to "the duty" of having one (everyone *must* have an opinion, says the journalist), what are the poor things to do! An opinion becomes an article of necessity for the general public—and here the journalist comes in and offers his assistance by peddling opinions. He works in a double capacity, first he propagandizes for all he is worth that every person should and must have an opinion—and then he recommends his wares: an assortment of opinions.

The journalist makes people ridiculous in two ways. First, by making them believe it is necessary to have an opinion, and that perhaps is the most ridiculous part of it: such a poor, good-natured burgher who could be so comfortable and whom the journalist now stuffs with the idea that it is necessary for him to have an opinion! Secondly, by hiring out an opinion which, despite its vapid consistence, is nevertheless put on and worn—as an article of necessity.

82.   *1844.*

What, after all, is Goethe in *Aus meinem Leben* other
than a talented defender of blunders? On no point
has he realized any idea, but he certainly knows how
to wheedle and prattle himself out of everything
(girls, the idea of passionate love, Christianity, etc.).
(*Marginal note*: And yet, if you will, all that does
not amount to much; he only differs in degree from
a criminal romancing his guilt away, "putting it at
a distance by writing." * S.K.)

83.   *1849.*

The writers in Denmark each got a copy of *Either-
Or.* * I felt it was my duty; and now I could do it; for
now there can't be any question at all about canvas-
sing it in that way, the book being old now, its crisis
past. Of course they received the copy from Victor
Eremita.* As to Oehlenschläger and Winther it gave
me a great joy to send them a copy, for I admire
them. As to Hertz, I also enjoyed doing it, for he is
of importance, and there also is something genial
about his mode of living.[1]

84.   *1844.*

If someone should wish to question the truth of the
saying that we are living in times when things are
moving, let him remember that Pastor Grundtvig
lives now, a man who far exceeds Archimedes and

---

[1] *Translator's note*: Victor Eremita was one of S. K.'s pseudonyms.
Adam Gottlob Oehlenschläger, Christian Winther and Henrik Hertz
were leading Danish writers.

does not need, nor dreams of needing, a fixed point in order to move heaven and earth, no indeed, he does it even without a foothold. So little does he need, or rather, he needs nothing, to bring about this tremendous effect, and being, in addition, capable of blowing up in fury, one will easily see that in our times things are not only moving, but it is truly disturbing to be the contemporaries of this "Nordic-beer" giant.[2]

85.   *1845.*

The small band of enthusiasts, formed in Grundtvig's "Nordic-beer" taproom.

86.   *1846.*

Like a basso who sometimes goes down so deep that his tone becomes inaudible, and only by standing very close to him one may notice certain convulsive motions about his mouth and throat proving that something *is* going on: thus Grundtvig sometimes gazes so deeply into History that he fails to show us anything; but it is deep, very deep!

87.   *1847.*

How very trivial the things are that have been written in the matter of the hymn-book.* To me the

---

[2] *Translator's note*: N. F. S. Grundtvig, later bishop, often was the object of S.K.'s barbs; when he calls him "beer-Nordic" it is a pun on the Danish "oldnordisk" (old Norse) and øl (beer). Grundtvig brought the Nordic myths and sagas back into Danish history-teaching.

hymn-singing is what engages me most in the entire service. For a hymn to be good I demand very simple and, in part, insignificant words (in which respect there are several in the evangelical hymn-book that are capital, exactly as they should be, and such as the swelling, turbulent Grundtvig could not possibly write) and then set to one of our moving, heartfelt tunes. I know Kingo's hymns by heart, but they are no good for singing, their contents being too forceful and their lyrics far too pretentious. Hymns like that one should read at home for edification.

But the piety which essentially is that of the silent sufferer (and this is the right kind), of *that* piety Grundtvig knows nothing at all. Grundtvig was, is and always will be a noise-maker; even in Eternity he will be unpleasing to me. Not that Grundtvig has not been through something; he has indeed; but always noisily.

Some item stops him in his tracks, whereupon he makes a big uproar, as if there had been a railway-collision. The deeper, inward pain, which in quiet sadness has made peace with God, is quite unknown to Grundtvig, and that is precisely the genuine note in hymn-singing. Grundtvig is either a yodeling whipper-snapper or a boisterous blacksmith.

How much deep feeling there is in a tune like "My heart now yearns."* Just as it would be impossible for me ever in all eternity to tire of looking at the sky in cloudy fall weather when the low, soft greys interweave in the most delicate tracings, so I could never tire of repeating the quiet rhythms of such a melody.

88.

Immortality   *1854.*

One of our poets (B. S. Ingemann) is said, sentimentally, to hold the opinion that even every insect is immortal.

The man is right, one is tempted to say, for if human beings as they are born today, *en masse*, are immortal, it would not seem unreasonable that insects also are.

It is this regular tea-party chatter, which is such sweet and touching unadulterated parson's twaddle, that always excels in sweetly diluting all concepts till they vanish into thin air, nay, become almost loathsome! Immortality, once the exalted goal to which the heroes of mankind looked up, humbly confessing that this reward was too overwhelming, that the reward bore no relation to their striving, strenuous though it was—and now every louse is immortal.

Verily, Ingemann should have been a parson, bound in velvet both front and back, with a gold tassel on his shoulder! Though I generally don't like to distort or make fun of a man's name, there really is something in Heiberg's pun on Ingemann's name when he calls him "Ingenmand" [in Danish this means: No man].

Oh, it is abominable, and it is particularly abominable that thousands of people take this to be fine sensitivity! May this knavish profession then take hold of the idea and those *"Gaudiebe"* [knaves], the parsons, manage to instil into "our Christian government" that something in the way of Christianity also ought to be done for the insects, these immortal creatures, that soul-shepherds ought to be appointed for them, or, at least, that some extra livings should be established.

2. GOLDSCHMIDT*

89.

*A Prayer to The Corsair**   *1845*.

Sing sang resches Tubalkain—which means: Oh, cruel, bloodthirsty Corsair, High and Mighty Sultan, thou who holdest men's lives like a prank in thy powerful hand and like a notion in the wrath [furious sneezing] of thy nose, oh, allow thyself to be moved to compassion, cut these sufferings short, kill me, but do not make me immortal! Most High and Mighty Sultan, reflect in thy instant wisdom what the most wretched of all those whom thou hast killed would soon be able to see, reflect so by attestation of *The Corsair*! Oh, what cruel mercy and salvation for all eternity: to be branded as an inhuman monster, because *The Corsair* inhumanly spared one! But above all, do not tell me that I shall never die. Perish the thought! Such a life penalty is unheard of! (*Marginal note*: Kill me that I may live with all the others thou hast killed, but do not kill me by making me immortal.) I became so weary of life merely by reading it. What a cruel distinction that no one shall be moved by my lament when it is sounded effeminately [?] like this: It will be the death of me, I shall take my death over it—and everyone then laughs saying: he cannot die.

Oh! suffer thyself to be moved by pity, put a halt to thy high, cruel grace, and kill me like all the rest.

Victor Eremita.

(Maybe one could add here the words at the end of the postscript in *Either-Or* which will be found in the narrow high-boy closest to the window.)

90.

It is now my idea to train myself for the ministry. These many months past I have prayed God to help me on my way, for it has long been clear to me that I ought not to continue as an author any longer; if I did I would want to be one completely, or not at all. That too is the reason why I have not begun on anything *New* simultaneously with my proof-reading, but only did the small review of the *Two Eras** which, incidentally, is of a terminal nature.

February 7, 1846.

91.   *1846.*

Now listen, little Corsair! Do be a man for once! It is effeminate to importune a man with one's infatuation; it is effeminate to continue to run after someone and pour abuse on him because of spurned love; be a man, keep silent. Only a woman, as a member of the weaker sex, might be forgiven for revealing her powerlessness first by urging her passionate abandon on a man and then, if rejected, by abandoning herself to naughty ill-temper; a man should be able to remain himself, to keep silent when he sees that it is an admission of impotence to continue heaping abuse on another exactly as when a woman is running

after a man, or an importunate beggar pursues him
up one street and down another.

92.   *1846.*

But nothing must be written;* not one word; I dare
not. What is written would yet suffice to give the
reader a hint and, to that extent, trouble him. It
must not be so that he learns something *sub rosa.* I
have thrown away a good deal lately that was not
badly written, but could only be used in an entirely
different context.

The last form I have imagined would be like this:

Brief and Pithy

As I see it, an editor is literally responsible if no
author is named. At *The Corsair* Mr. Undergraduate
Goldschmidt is editor, a bright head, without ideas,
without studies, without views, without self-control,
but not without a certain talent and esthetically desperate force. At a critical moment of his life he
turned* to me; I indirectly sought to support him
negatively: I praised him for having made a secure
position for himself. I believe he has succeeded in
getting what he wanted. I had hoped he would have
chosen the path of honor for achieving a name; in
all sincerity, it pains me that as editor of *The Corsair*
he continues to choose the path of contemptibleness
in order to earn money. My wish was, if possible to
tear away a nevertheless intelligent person from becoming a tool of vulgarity. (*Marginal note*: No Dane
can put up with a situation where Vulgarity possesses
an organ with a very wide circulation, at whose mercy
he will be if it so should please a literary lazzarone.)

But verily it was not my wish to receive ignominious wages in the guise of being immortalized by a gazette of contemptibleness that ought never to exist, and by which I only can wish to be lambasted. It suits my writer's existence to be lambasted, that is why I wished it and demanded it immediately when I had finished, for at the time *Frater Taciturnus* was writing, *Johannes Climacus** had already been delivered to the printer's some days before. Moreover, it had been my hope that I might be of some use to others by this step; they did not want that, very well then, I shall continue to demand that they heap abuse on me because it suits my idea and thus, at least, I shall derive some benefit from the fact that such a sheet exists. It is sad indeed to see the great number of fools and injudicious persons who laugh, and in this matter do not even know what they are laughing at. Only God knows if I am not playing for too high stakes in relation to my contemporaries; my idea demands it; its consistency gratifies me indescribably —I cannot do otherwise. I beg the forgiveness of those better men who are not dialectical nor have the presuppositions to understand that I have to act like this; and then—*en avant*—let me be lambasted! No matter how significant or insignificant my life as a writer is, this much is certain: I am the only Danish writer who, by dint of my dialectical relation, is in the precise position that it can suit his idea that all kinds of lies, distortions, galimatias and calumnies come to the fore to disturb the reader and thus impel him to think for himself, independently, and prevent the direct relation [dependency]. No other Danish author could possibly be served by a state of affairs

where addressing himself to 100 readers, lies and
distortions find 1000 readers. But Goldschmidt ren-
ders me a service every time he serves up abuse of
me; and he will surely keep it up; he cannot do without me, and his inability to pursue the good is expressed in defiance of an unhappy infatuation and a
deafening of his own self by harsh abuse which, in
a way, should make me feel sorry for him, as I meant
well by him. His lambasting me on the contrary, is
none of my concern. I can very well absent myself.

If Mr. Goldschmidt will make a signed reply in a
decent paper I shall read it; I no longer read *The
Corsair*. I wouldn't even give it to my servant to read,
for I do not think it is within a master's competence
to direct his servant to frequent an indecent place.

S.K.

93.   1847.

Being trampled to death by geese is a slow way of
dying, and letting oneself be torn and worn to death
by envy also is a long-drawn-out process. While the
mob derides me (for what appears once in a gazette
does not really mean much if it were not a signal for
all the rabble henceforth day after day to mock and
abuse one in public thoroughfares; school-boys, flippant undergraduates, shop-assistants, and all the rabble dredged up by vulgar literature, are regarded
with approbation by the envious high-ranking world)
they think it serves me well. And under such conditions one should want to live, or bother to live! No,
but at least I am happy in the knowledge that I have
acted. However, such gnawing maltreatment chafes

most painfully. Everything else finally comes to an end, but this thing will never cease. To sit in church and have a couple of impudent louts sit down beside one and constantly stare at one's trousers and ridicule one by their remarks which they exchange so loudly that every word can be heard. Still, I am quite used to such things. The fact that impudence finds a stronghold in a gazette makes the brazen ones believe they are completely in the right, nay, that they are the standard-bearers of public opinion. And of course, so it is; in a certain sense I am still mistaken about Denmark; I still did not believe that vulgarity constituted Denmark's true public opinion, but I shall testify to it with pleasure, and it is actually easy to prove.

94.   *1847.*

How disgusting is the tyranny of grossness and vulgarity that prevails in Copenhagen, what nauseous dissolution; one does not feel it so much because each individual only contributes his own small share. But when the few better ones, meanly looking out for their own advantage, always cede the way, hide under mama's skirts and in the bosom of the family, and sneak away to some hide-away of the higher circles, then it is never discovered. That is why I will stand firm, fully conscious of what I am doing while "superior brains" think I am crazy. Men are not wicked, but led astray; the thing is to call their attention to it. The day when the rabble in this city will pull my hat over my ears, (and that day may not be far distant) on that day I shall have triumphed. Then everyone will see the abomination it leads to and also see my crime for what it was: that I was the only one who had sufficient courage to make myself deserving in the good cause. Danes are the most craven cowards, maybe not so much in war as when it comes to their shyness [fear of stepping forward in a cause]. The Danish people are almost no longer a nation, but a herd like the Jews, Copenhagen no metropolis, but a regular small town.

95.   1847.

There is a form of envy of which I frequently have seen examples, in which an individual tries to obtain something by bullying. If, for instance, I enter a place where many are gathered, it often happens that one or another right away takes up arms against me by beginning to laugh; presumably he feels that he is being a tool of public opinion. But lo and behold, if I then make a casual remark to him, that same person becomes infinitely pliable and obliging. Essentially it shows that he regards me as something great, maybe even greater than I am: but if he can't be admitted as a participant in my greatness at least he will laugh at me. But as soon as he becomes a participant, as it were, he brags about my greatness.

That is what comes of living in a petty community,
One day outside the gate I met three young gentlemen who, as soon as they caught sight of me, began to grin and altogether initiated the whole gamut of insolence that is *bon ton* in our small town here. What happens? When I was near enough to see them distinctly I noticed that they were all smoking cigars, so I turned to one of them and asked for a light. but it is extremely interesting to observe.

Then, instantly, all three doffed their hats and it would seem I had done them a service by asking for a light. *Ergo*: the same people would be happy to cry *bravo* for me if I merely address a friendly, let alone, flattering word to them; as it is, they cry *pereat** [he shall perish!] and are defiant.

What Goldschmidt and P. L. Møller practice in a big way, everyone here does on a smaller scale. If one neglects to salute Goldschmidt or does not want to call on him, then he puts you in his paper. He tries to obtain equality by bullying. The same goes for the readers of his sheet. If you refuse to flatter them they use his sheet to mock you; if you flatter them their true judgment comes to the fore.

And I who always have been politeness incarnate, particularly toward the less privileged classes! Now all it amounts to is play-acting. But how invaluably interesting to have one's knowledge of human psychology enriched in this way.

96.

Perhaps after all this deserves to be noted down.

1849.

Goldschmidt (apart from his general lack of character and his baseness) never has had ideas, though he probably had talent. Under his editorship *The Corsair* never was without talent, and so it will not be forgotten on that account.

Now, as I happened to see, he says in *"North and South,"** where he is defending his activity, that considering the shabbiness of the parties he took an ironical stand to them.

The long and the short of it is this: Was *The Corsair* to have ideas, and if so, it would depend upon and would have to be tested against whether it had dialectics enough to stand pat and sufficient personal courage to express absolute negativity.*

Of such things Goldschmidt had not the faintest idea. *The Corsair* was liberal and made Christian VIII, officialdom, etc. its whipping boys. *The Corsair* was an outgrowth of opposition. Goldschmidt never had any ideas.

Some time ago then I gave Goldschmidt a small hint to the effect that, apart from the immorality of the phenomenon, if there were to be any question at all of an Idea in this or in any similar enterprise, it should aim equally at everything and not, in our times, be so stupid as to direct its barbs solely against the government. This hint was given *en passant*, with all the distant reserve I always observed with him.

My idea in taking this step was, in regard to Goldschmidt, the following:

1) Either, in relation to eternity, he must come to judge himself eternally, see that he has absolutely no character and that he even despises himself. That happened.

2) Or he answers: No, a writer's work which I have admired and said that I admired, I can certainly not, since it has not changed, turn round and scoff at; I am only referring to the little article in *The Fatherland*.

3) Or he could have said: No, I do not attack *Magister* Kierkegaard.

In the last contingency it would have been my intention to sit in judgment a little. For the sake of calling the public's attention to the precipice they had skirted I would have demonstrated (by attacking faked names, that is, and entirely without any sting, purely esthetically) how such things should have been managed and, in addition, how dangerous it could become if the people in question were real persons.

After that my idea was to have Goldschmidt removed and placed as esthetic columnist on decent conditions with a decent periodical. He has a bright head; actually, he was the only younger man I had noticed. He might then have become useful to me in the esthetic field.

That would have been most beneficial to him. He needs such an influence. As is now evident, he can very well make a way for himself, obtain many subscribers, etc., but his life will always lack a central idea.

The test to which he was submitted was strictly carried out. The same day on which the article about P. L. Møller appeared, (or the day after), he accosted me in the street, evidently with the intention of making me tell him privately what I wanted him to do. That I did not; I even treated him coldly.

Then, the next day, when the whole cart-load of abuse had been heaped on me, I met him in the street. He passed me by; I called to him: Goldschmidt. He came up to me. Then I told him to walk along with me. I said that perhaps after all he had misunderstood everything I had put before him when I admonished him to give up his *Corsair* activity, that perhaps he had been harboring the illusion that I kept up appearances with him to avoid becoming

the butt of his attacks. Now I hoped he could see
that the contrary was the case. I therefore wanted to
repeat very earnestly what I had told him. I did so.
I put it to him very earnestly that he must leave *The
Corsair*. It was both ludicrous and pathetic when,
with tears in his eyes (he is the kind of person that
weeps easily) he said: To think that you could judge
my whole conduct like that and not say one word
about my having some talent after all.

Having said my piece, I doffed my hat and bade
him farewell in the benevolent, but distant, manner
I have always observed with him.

Since then I never have spoken with him again.
In truth, it is not because of *my* feelings: not only
do I forgive him for what he has done to me, but I
am not the least bit angry about it; I am not so in-
consistent. No, I felt I owed it to the circumstances.
I was still always considered "the man of irony"; if
after the event, I had kept up appearances with him
it would have meant a tremendous support of him,
meant that I sanctioned the interpretation that his
goings-on were irony. Easy-going as I am it has been
a real strain on me to act the part of "the angry
man."

97.   January 24, *(1847)*

God be praised that all those attacks of the rabble*
came upon my head. I now have had time truly to
study my inner being and make sure that, after all,
it was a melancholy idea this wanting to live in some
far-away parsonage in order to do penance in remoteness and oblivion. Now I stand pat, much more determined than ever before. And if this torrent of deri-

sion had not been poured on me I should have been
pursued for ever by that melancholy idea, for a
certain form of good fortune actually is favorable to
the breeding of melancholy ideas; thus, for instance,
if I had not had private means, despite all my native
bent toward melancholia, I should never have fallen
into it as deeply as has sometimes been the case.

V

PHILOSOPHY AND SCIENCE

1. CONTEMPORARY PHILOSOPHY

98.   *1842.*

All the many tutors, private lecturers and survey-compilers who in today's Germany take it upon themselves to acquaint people with philosophy and to expound its present position are as loathsome to me, with all their unfeeling newspapers reports about the state of philosophy, as the sleepy, indolent bil-liard-markers with their monotonous cry: *dixe a ons* [sic!] Yet, strangely enough, philosophy advances con-stantly, and that despite the fact that among the whole caboodle of philosophers there is not a single player, only markers. In vain I wait for a man to step forward endowed with the power to say: à point! In vain; we are already far along in *quarant* [sic]; the game will soon be over and all mysteries solved. If, at least, the German philosophers could explain the mystery that the game goes on, though no one is playing! Is it any wonder then that, with matters as they are in Germany, I stake my hope on Danish phi-losophy. My barber too, an elderly, but knowledge-able man, who has followed the recent stirrings of

Danish philosophy with vivid interest, maintains that Denmark never has had such philosophers as today, unless it be at the very beginning. The other day he was good enough to spend the ten minutes he usually devotes to shaving off my beard, to giving me a brief survey of newer Danish philosophy. He assumes it to start with *Riegels,* *Horrebov and Boie.** Riegels he has known very closely; he was his friend and close pal, a small stocky man, always happy and cheerful. My barber clearly remembers what a sensation Riegels made when he appeared on the scene. He asserted several excellent truths. My barber had forgotten what these truths were; many years have gone by now; but he certainly remembers as vividly as if it were yesterday, what a sensational impression Riegels produced. *Horrebov* and *Boie* always frequented his barbershop, so he had every opportunity of delving into their philosophies. These three men must be considered the protagonists of recent Danish philosophy. Also *Riisbright,** although in his quiet, less conspicuous activity as lecturer at the University of Copenhagen, should be mentioned here. Yet, all in all, he remained on the fringe of the great movements in recent Danish philosophy. But what my barber could not help recalling with deep pathos was that Denmark should lose so early the most gifted philosophical brain she ever possessed. This man is now forgotten; many may not even know that he ever existed. His name was *Niels Rasmussen*, and he was a contemporary of the three great philosophers. He had conceived the brilliant idea that all European philosophies should rally round Danish philosophy and this, in turn, round his own. With this in mind he worked hard on a subscription plan, but it required so much of his strength that he died from overwork. If, said my barber, *if* this subscription plan had been carried through, if the work it advertized had been finished, if it had been read, if it had been translated, if it had been understood by the European philosophers, then the promising Niels Rasmussen without any doubt would have raised Denmark to a point of eminence which even now it has not attained. However, he died, Denmark's philosophical hope! The barber and I shed a tear for the deceased, whereupon he went on shaving my beard and giving me a survey of recent Danish philosophy. What Riegels had confided to him in a moment of mirth, what Horrebov, Boie and he had tattled about in the barbershop was circulated throughout the land and rumored abroad. He stopped for a moment to whisk off some soap-lather, using the pause to show me on a map suspended on the wall how recent Danish philosophy, in its eminent expansion, had covered Sealand, penetrated far north into Norway, right up to Trondhjem. Everyone was justified in expecting something extraordinary to come of these stirrings, but then the unfortunate war years came and crushed out everything. However, he had now regained courage and was hoping anew. The present epoch in Danish philosophy easily proved to bear an essential relation to the preceding epoch in recent Danish philosophy; it touched it, and only left its result to find a loftier one. The former epoch worked toward sound human reason and found it; the present epoch tends to abandon this relative superficiality in order to attain something Higher. It may have discovered that there is something else and

more important, something which, until further notice, it calls the innermost back of existence or what
is behind the innermost of existence! As soon as our
present-day philosophy has found out what this is or,
as my barber expressed it more correctly, manages to
get behind it, Danish philosophy will attain the European renown Niels Rasmussen intended it to have.
This, my barber opines, one can mostly certainly
hope for, fully confident of its extraordinary forces.

99. 1844.

If Hegel had written his entire Logic and said in the
preface that it was merely an idea-experiment for the
sake of argument, wherein even in many places he
had shirked* something, he might well have been
the greatest thinker that ever lived. As it is, he is
comical.

100.

All in all, one must say that recent philosophy, even
in its most grandiose presentation, still essentially is
merely an introduction offering a possibility for philosophizing. *Hegel** undeniably terminates, but only
the development that got under way with Kant* and
which was directed at cognition; through Hegel we
have arrived, in a deeper form, at the result which
the preceding philosophers* used directly as a start-
ing-point, i.e. that there is any reality at all in thinking; but the whole thinking which, taking off from
this direct point (or happy about this result), entered into the essential anthropological contemplation,* *that* is something which the philosophers have
not yet tackled. July 5, 1840.

101.   *1843.*

Despite all protestations as to the positivity inherent
in Hegel's system he still has only arrived at the point
where formerly philosophy started (e.g., Leibnitz.*).

102.
The System   1854.

Personality is the Aristocratic—system, however, is a
plebeian invention; a system (that omnibus) is a
vehicle that permits everybody to ride along.

That is why in the lingo of thieves, which always
turns things upside down, it is said: he was only a
personality, he had no system—that is, the Lower is
turned into the Higher.

103.   *1846.*

It is with most systematicians in relation to their systems as with a man who has built a vast palace and
himself occupies a barn close by: they do not themselves live in their vast systematic structures. But in
matters of the mind and spirit this is and remains
a definite objection. Spiritually speaking a man's
thoughts must inhabit the house in which he lives
—or else there is something wrong.

104.
Hegel   1851.

What was more honest in former days about even the
most embittered attacks on Christianity was that there
was approximate acceptance of what Christianity *is*.

The most dangerous thing about Hegel* is that he has modified Christianity—and thereby made it conform to his philosophy.

That is altogether characteristic of the age of reason: not to leave the problem as it is and say No, but to alter the problem and then say: Yes, by all means, we are in agreement.

The hypocrisy of reason is infinitely sly. That is why it is so hard to catch sight of.

105.

For long, long periods the human race worried about the question of God as a Personality. If only *that* could be apprehended, people imagined that the Trinity* might be left in abeyance.

What happened? Hegel and the Hegelians arrived. They understood the matter better: they proved that God was a person precisely because of His being tri-une. Well, thank you! That set things right. All the business about a Trinity was a sham—it was merely the old logical trilogy (thesis—antithesis—synthesis) and the resulting "Personality" was approximately the "X" with which one started out in those days when people thought that if they could only succeed in comprehending God's personality, the Trinity could be left pending.

Altogether, the most profound confusion of the Hegelian concept in relation to the Christian concept is that the Hegelian has no time and no head for *first* positing the Christian problem before comprehension can be achieved. Hegel's results (announced with kettle-drums and trumpets as explaining Everything) approximately represent the problem as it shapes up:

the problem we are trying to comprehend, or to comprehend that we cannot comprehend it.

Hegel ends about where Christianity begins; but there is this misunderstanding that Hegel believes he has reached the end *at that point*, nay that he has come much farther.

As for me, I simply cannot help laughing whenever I think of Hegel's comprehension of Christianity, for indeed it is something extremely incomprehensible. And what I have always said is and remains true: Hegel was a professor of philosophy, not a thinker; moreover, he must have been a rather insignificant personality without real life-experience, but I certainly do not deny that he was a most extraordinary professor.

I wonder if the day will not come when this concept of "professor" will come to equate a comic person. Just think of Christianity! Alas, how different it is from the age when it had inflexible confessors and the day when it got flexible professors [declinable] in all *casibus*.

[A pun: in Danish to *decline* (*cases*) is to bend, flex, *make pliable*.]

106.
Somewhere in my dissertation   1850.

Influenced as I was by Hegel and all the Modern thinking, not mature enough properly to grasp the Great, there is a place* in my dissertation where I could not help showing it up as an imperfection in Socrates that he had no eye for Totality but, numerically, only saw Individuals.

Oh, what a Hegelian fool I was; this precisely provides the great evidence of what a great teacher of ethics Socrates was.

107. *1844.*

Who has forgotten that fine Easter Morning* when Professor Heiberg arose and grasped the Hegelian philosophy in the way he himself so edifyingly explained: was it not by a leap?* Or did somebody dream that up?

108. *1843.*

Heiberg, in his outcry* about *Either-Or,* observed that there were remarks in it of which one did not quite know whether they were profound or not. That is the great advantage Professor Heiberg and his associates enjoy: one knows beforehand, before one hears it, that what they have to say is profound. The reason is partly that one rarely or never comes across a single original thought in them. What they know they have borrowed from Hegel. And Hegel, we know, is profound—*ergo* what Professor Heiberg says is profound. In this way every student of Divinity who in his sermon confines himself to quotations from the Bible becomes the most profound of them all; for of all books the Bible surely is the most profound.

109. *1843.*

Maybe Professor Heiberg feels that Christianity is a subject for a musical play.[1]

---

[1] *Translator's note*: H. was known for his plays with interspersed songs, at the time known as "vaudevilles."

110.   [no date]

I now see that, basically, Professor Heiberg and I
agree that he is right in the principal matter, for what
matters most is that he has satisfied the demand of
the times by his gilt New Year's present.* The only
thing we differ about is our opinion as to what *is* the
demand of the times. Professor Heiberg thinks it is
astronomy.* That I doubt. My opinion is that our
times demand a most elegant, neat and tidy book in
gilt binding with as little as possible printed on each
page, or, to express myself more succinctly: what our
times demand is to be gulled and led by the nose.† In
that sense Professor Heiberg has gratified the demand
of the times by his gilt New Year's gift.

   † That this really continues to be the demand of
the times can be proved by innumerable examples; on
the other hand the professor is the only person to
have discovered that astronomy was what our times
demanded.

111.   *1843.*

It is also the wont of Prof. Heiberg to "hold judg-
ment-day in literature"; have you forgotten what happened to Xerxes? He even had brought scribes along
to record his victory over little Greece.

112.   *1843.*

For several years now Prof. Heiberg has been sitting
at the window of literature waving his hand at the
passers-by, especially if there was a splendid personage among them and he heard a little hurrah from
the neighboring street.

113.   *1843.*

Prof. Heiberg is a peculiar man
veet-teh—veet—veet—bom—bom.

S.K.

2. SETTLING ACCOUNTS WITH PHYSICAL SCIENCE

114.   *1846.*

Of all sciences physical science is decidedly the most insipid, and I find it amusing to reflect how, with the passing of time, that becomes trite which once called forth amazement, for such is the invariable lot of the discoveries inherent in "the bad Infinity."* Just remember what a stir it made when the Stethoscope* was introduced. Soon we shall have reached the point where every barber will use it and, when shaving you, will ask: Would you like to be stethoscoped, Sir? Then someone else will invent an instrument for listening to the beats of the brain. That will make a tremendous stir until, in 50 years, every barber can do it. Then in a barbershop, when one has had a haircut and a shave and has been stethoscoped (for by then it will be very common) the barber will ask: Perhaps you would also like me to listen to your brain-beats?

115.   *1846.*

It is simple and beautiful and moving when a lover looks lovingly at his beloved, but it is most distinguished to gaze at her through opera-glasses. And so the physicist uses the microscope as a dandy uses opera-glasses; only, the microscope is focused on God.

116.   *1846.*

If by means of research in the natural sciences something could be found that would help to define the
concept of mind and spirit, I would be the first to
acquire a microscope, and I hope I should be as perse-
vering as anyone. However, as I easily perceive by
qualitative dialectic* that, qualitatively understood,
the world will not have advanced another step in
100,000 years, I will do precisely the opposite: preserve my soul and not waste one second of my life on
curiosity. Then when some day I am lying on my
deathbed I shall derive comfort from saying: I have
certainly not understood the least little thing of that
sort, not understood the least bit more than my man
Anders* or a servant maid; only, I may have praised
God more often, wonderingly and worshipfully. I
quite well understand that it is God who has given
man that kind of acute intellect that permits him to
invent instruments and the like, but since it is also
God who has given man the mind that permits him,
by qualitative dialectic,* to see the self-contradiction
inherent in this quantitative, approximating* "AL-
MOST," man ought piously and humbly to give up
curiosity, leave behind the sort of spiritual immobil-
ity necessary for microscopical observation and, instead, worship God and maintain relations with him
only through the Ethical.

117.   *1846.*

It is no use at all to tangle with the natural sciences.
There one is defenseless and cannot exercise any con-

trol. The researcher right away begins dissipating his brain on details: now someone is going to Australia, now to the moon, now into a subterranean cavern, now the Devil knows where in the arse after an intestinal worm;* now we must have a telescope, now a microscope: who in the name of Satan can stand it!

But, joking aside, let me speak seriously. The confusion lies in this: that it never becomes dialectically clear what is what, *how* philosophy is to make use of natural science. Is the whole thing an ingenious image-language (so that one might just as well remain ignorant of it); is it example, analogy; or is it of such importance that a new theory must be adapted in relation to it?

For a thinker there cannot exist any anguish more horrible than having to live on in tension while detail upon detail is being accumulated, and all the time it looks as if *the idea, the conclusion,* would come the next time. If the physicist does not feel this anguish he cannot be a thinker. That is the terrible tantalus-torment of the intellectual! A thinker feels as if he is in Hell as long as he has not reached that certainty of the spirit: *hic Rhodus, hic salta,* the sphere of faith in which all that matters is that, even if the whole world explodes and the elements dissolve, you *must believe*! Here we don't wait for official news by mail nor for shipping communications. This certainty of the spirit, the most humble of all, the most offensive to the vain mind (for it is so very distinguished to peer through a microscope) is the only true certainty.

The principal objection, the total objection to the

natural sciences, can formally be expressed simply and
definitely like this: It is unthinkable that it could
occur to a human being who has reached a conclusion about himself as a spirit in relation to eternity,
to choose physical science (with its empirical material) as a field for his efforts. An observant physicist
must *either* be a man of talent-and-instinct (for the
special characteristic of talent-and-instinct is not to
be dialectical deep down, but only to be able to use
flair, be ingenious—however *not* to understand itself)
(*Marginal note*: and to be able to live on blissfully
in that way without any feeling of precariousness, because the deceptive multiplicity of observations and
discovery constantly cover up the total lack of clarity)
or he must be someone who, from an earlier youth,
almost unbeknownst to himself, has become a physicist, and then became accustomed to living in that
way—the most horrible way of life: i.e. to captivate
and astound the entire world with his discoveries and
and ingeniousness, and then not to understand his
own self! That such a physicist has a consciousness
goes without saying, he has a consciousness within
the circumscribed scope of his talent, perhaps he has
amazing acumen, a gift of combination, almost a
conjuror's knack for idea-associations, and so on. But
at the very maximum it amounts to this: such an
eminent talent, this absolutely uniquely gifted man
is able to explain Nature, but does not understand
his own self! He does not become transparent to himself in regard to his spiritual destiny, to the ethical
guidance of his talent, etc. But this state of affairs is
nothing but scepticism, as is easily seen (for scepti-

sicm is this: that an unknown quantity, some "X," can explain everything. But when everything is explained through an "X" which is not explained, then *in toto* nothing is explained, nothing at all. If this is not scepticism, then it is superstition.

118. *1846.*

By way of the natural sciences a most tragic dividing line will arise between simple people, who believe simply, and scholars and pseudo-scholars who have gazed through a microscope. No longer will one dare, as in olden times, openheartedly to address one's words about the simple Highest to all, all, all people, whether they be black or green, whether they have big heads or small: no, one must first look and see if they have brains enough to believe in God. If Christ had known about the microscope, he would have examined the apostles before accepting them.

119. *1846.*

Let us take such problems as freedom* i.e. free will and necessity.* Then let the physiologist begin to explain all about how, if the blood circulates in a certain way, this and that is influenced, the same with pressure on the nerves, etc. etc.—yet in the end he cannot explain that freedom is an illusion. After having written 4 folios full of figures and curiosities he must say: but at the ultimate question our wonders stop. Then to what end all this knowledge? Is it not in inmost truth to deceive a human being, and is it not tantamount to gradually tricking him out of enthusiasm and keeping him suspended in the false expectation that sometime, by means of still more powerful microscopes, one would succeed in finding out that freedom had been an illusion, that the whole thing was a function of natural science?

All knowledge has something captivating about it; but on the other hand it changes the state of soul of the one who has it. The objectivity, the lack of interest, with which a physiologist counts a person's pulse-beats, or studies his nerves, have no relation to ethical enthusiasm. And finally when the physiologist has filled his 4 extremely curious folios with the most astounding observations, he will admit to himself, if he be truly honest and spiritual, that he has not explained the Ultimate: the Ultimate which is the First and the Last of Ethics. And after the reader has finished the 4 folios and admired the physiologist, his state of mind will have undergone a gradual change. Do not, therefore, say that the Ethical shuns the light, is obscurantist, etc.—no—but the Ethical is hostile to a body of knowledge which, after having consumed a man's whole life, ultimately ends in his not being able to explain the most important.

Let us picture the biggest criminal that ever lived and imagine that physiology by then has been able to find a pair of even more splendid spectacles to put on its nose than at present, so that it could explain why this man was a criminal: that the whole thing was a necessity of Nature, that his brain was too small, etc.—how horrible that acquittal, freeing him of further investigation, would be in comparison with the judgment Christianity pronounces on him, namely that, unless he mends his evil ways, he will go down to Hell.

3. THE INDIVIDUAL—THE CROWD

120.   *1846.*

One can very well eat lettuce before its heart has been formed; still, the delicate crispness of the heart and its lovely frizz are something altogether different from the leaves. It is the same in the world of the spirit. Being too busy has this result: that an individual very, very rarely is permitted to form a heart; on the other hand, the thinker, the poet, or the religious personality who actually has formed his heart, will never be popular, not because he is difficult, but because it demands quiet and prolonged working with oneself and intimate knowledge of oneself as well as a certain isolation. Even if, in a full-toned voice, I could say something that would please each and every one, if it were of a religious nature I would not say it, because it is already a kind of religious indecency that it should be necessary to make an outcry about it; on the contrary, religious things have to do with a softly murmured soliloquy with oneself. Alas, things are so topsy-turvy that, instead of having to do with each individual going alone into his secret closet to commune quietly with himself, people believe that religion is a matter for very loud talk.

121.   *1847.*

I am accused of causing young people to acquiesce in subjectivity. Maybe, for a moment. But how would it be possible to eliminate all the phantoms of objectivity* that act as an audience, etc., except by stressing the category of the separate individual.* Under the pretext of objectivity the aim has been to sacrifice

individualities entirely. That is the crux of the
matter.

<h2 style="text-align:center">122.   1847.</h2>

The evolution of the whole world tends* to show the
absolute importance of the category of the individual
apart from the crowd which precisely is the Christian
principle. But as yet we have not come very far concretely, though it is recognized *in abstracto.** That
explains why it still impresses people as prideful and
overweening arrogance to speak of the separate individual, whereas this precisely is truly human: each
and every one is an individual. Sometimes the misunderstanding is expressed piously. Thus when the
late Bishop Møller of Lolland said (in the introduction to his *Guidance*) that it would indeed be sad if
truth *(in specie* [in this case] Christianity) were accessible only to a few individuals and not to All: certainly
he said something true, but at the same time something false, for Christianity certainly is accessible to
all, but—note this well—thereby and solely that each
of us becomes an individual, becomes a separate person. But neither this ethical nor religious courage is
available as yet. Most people become quite afraid
when each is expected to be a separate individual.
Thus the matter turns and revolves upon itself. One
moment a man is supposed to be arrogant, setting
forth this view of the individual, and the next, when
the individual is about to carry it out in practice,
the idea is found to be much too big, too overwhelming, for him.

123. *1848.*

Each human being has infinite reality, and it is pride and arrogance in a person not to honor his fellow-man. Oh, if I could speak in that vein to every single human being I am convinced I should be able to move him. But it is a paralogism [false deduction] that one thousand human beings are worth more than one; that would be tantamount to regarding men as animals. The central point about being human is that the unit "1" is the highest; "1000" counts for less.

Alas, alas, alas—until one gets people trained in that dialectic.

124.

Being Alone *1854.*

The yardstick for a human being is: how long and to what degree he can bear to be alone, devoid of understanding with others.

A man who could bear being alone during a whole life-time, and alone in decisions of eternal significance, is farthest removed from the infant and the society-person who represent the animal-definition of a human being.

125.

The Collision in Human Existence *1854.*

Between being spiritual man and merely brute man, there is a big qualitative difference.

But this difference is not discernible to the senses.

The collision comes because brute men rush in on a spiritual man, or are set upon him like hounds. If I were to describe this in Greek I would have to say that this spectacle amuses the gods as hunting to hounds amuses men. Actually, it is more amusing, because what it is all about from the viewpoint of the senses is nothing. And considered as a hunting-to-hounds this fight is also more grandiose than an ordinary hunt, for what are some hundreds of hounds compared with these legions of brute men.

From a Christian point of view the matter presents a different aspect; there the collision constitutes the education of the spiritual man, his graduation, and also his mission, as his task includes testifying to the fact that man is spirit which, with the passing centuries, as polished brutishness mounts, becomes increasingly necessary, but also requires increasingly greater effort.

126.

"The crowd" is essentially what I am aiming my polemical arrow at; and it was Socrates who taught me to do so. I want people to sit up and take notice, to prevent them from idling away and wasting their lives. Aristocrats take it for granted that a lot of people will always go to waste. But they keep silent about it; they live sheltered lives pretending that all these many, many people simply do not exist. That is what is ungodly about the superior status of the aristocrats: in order to be comfortable themselves they do not even call attention to anything.

I will not be like that. I will call the attention of the crowd to their own ruination. And if they don't want to see it willingly, I shall make them see it by fair means or foul. Please understand me—or, at least, do not misunderstand me. I do not intend to beat them (alas, one man cannot beat the crowd); no, I will force them to beat me. Thus I actually compel them. For if they begin to beat me, they will probably pay attention; and if they kill me, they most definitely will pay attention, and I shall have won an absolute victory. In that respect I am a complete composite of dialectics. Already now many a person says: "Who cares about *Magister* Kierkegaard! I'll show him, you just wait and see!" Alas, but showing that they don't care about me, or caring that I should know they don't care about me, still denotes dependence. That fits in beautifully, provided one has sufficient ataraxia* [imperturbability]. They show me respect precisely by showing me that they don't respect me. Men are not so corrupt that they actually wish to do evil, but they are blinded, and don't really know what they are doing. It is all a matter of baiting them for decisive action. A child may long to be more or less defiant of his father, but if the father can only make it commit a real onslaught, the child is much closer to being saved. The rebellion of a crowd triumphs if one cedes the way, steps aside, so that it never comes to realize what it is doing. A crowd has no essential viewpoint; therefore if it happens to kill a man it is *eo ipso* halted; it pays heed and comes to its senses.

He, who for purposes of reformation, opposes a man of power (a pope, an emperor, in brief, a man who stands alone) must endeavor to make the mighty one fall, but he who more rightly turns round to

combat the "crowd," from which all corruption issues, must seek his own fall.

127.

The Individual—the Crowd—for God   1850.

The great thing about Socrates was that even when
he was accused and faced the People's Assembly, his
eyes did not see the crowd, but only the individual.

Spiritual superiority only sees the individual. But,
alas, ordinarily we human beings are sensual and,
therefore, as soon as it is a gathering, the impression
changes—we see something abstract, the crowd, and
we become different.

But in the eyes of God, the infinite spirit, all the
millions that have lived and now live do not make
a crowd, He only sees each individual.

128.

Majority—Minority.   *1850.*

Truth always rests with the minority, and the minority is always stronger than the majority, because
the minority is generally formed by those who really
have an opinion, while the strength of a majority is
illusory, formed by the gangs who have no opinion
—and who, therefore, in the next instant (when it is
evident that the minority is the stronger) assume *its*
opinion, which then becomes that of the majority,
i.e., becomes nonsense by having the whole train and
numerus [big numbers] on its side, while Truth
again reverts to a new minority.

In regard to Truth, this troublesome monster, the
majority, the public, etc., fares in the same way as

we say of someone who is traveling to regain his health: he is always one station behind.

129.

The Individual—Numbers [numerus]   *1854.*

Nobody wants to be this strenuous thing: an individual; it demands an effort. But everywhere services are readily offered through the phony substitute: a few! Let us get together and be a gathering, then we can probably manage. Therein lies mankind's deepest demoralization.

130.

Impotence—Power   *1854.*

According to the contemporary concept I am, of all people, the most powerless, not only not a member of a big party, let alone a small party, but not even a member of a party of two.

And yet on the contemporary scene I am definitely the only one that represents power—for numbers (as a concept) mean impotence, the bigger the more powerless.

131.

Gigantic Enterprises   *1854.*

Alas, what a change! Once upon a time it was so that a gigantic enterprise made one think of one man: a giant.

Nowadays they brag of gigantic enterprises, but when you come down to it these really are dwarf-enterprises, a couple of million dwarfs joined, and the crux is precisely their great number.

4. EXISTENCE—REDUPLICATION

132.   1846.

Stuff and nonsense and balderdash instead of action, that is really what people want; then they find things interesting. Goethe* tells in *"Aus Meinem Leben"* that "Werthers Leiden" [the sufferings of young Werther] produced such a sensation that ever since, he never could obtain the tranquillity and seclusion needed to lose himself in thought as before, for success carried him into all sorts of relationships and connections. How interesting and touching it is to chat! Nothing could have been easier than preventing it, if Goethe in truth had had courage, if, in truth, he had loved thinking better than acquaintances; a man with a strength like Goethe's can easily keep people at arm's length. But lo and behold, being soft and tenderhearted he will not do that, but he will tell about it as an event. And that is the kind of thing people love to listen to, for it dispenses them from acting. If someone would preach thus: "Once upon a time, in my early youth, I really possessed faith, in tranquil peace; but then I got busy in the world of society; there were so many acquaintances and I became a titular Councilor of Justice, and since then I actually never have had time for thought or concentration"—then people would find such a speech touching and would fain listen to it. The secret of life, if one wants to get on well, is: plenty of chit-chat about what one intends to do and how one is kept from doing it—and no action.

One day State Councilor Molbech* called on me. He praised my peculiarity and my special way of living, because it favored my chances to work. "I want to do the same," he said. Then he went on to tell me that he was going to a dinner-party the same day and "there I shall have to drink wine, and that does not agree with me, but it is impossible to avoid, for if I refuse, I immediately must hear: 'Oh, just a small glass, Mr. State Councilor; it is good for you.' " I replied "Nothing is easier than to prevent this. Don't breathe a word about wine not agreeing with you, for if you do, you yourself will provoke the loquacious sympathy. Just sit down, and, when the wine is being poured sniff its bouquet and say, or show by your facial expression, that the wine is not good. That will vex the host, and he will not press you." To this Molbech replied: "No, I can't do that; why should I fall out with people?" I answered: "To carry out your intention—is that not a sufficient reason?" But that is how it is: first prattle for an hour about it to me and make a fool of me with such flatulent insipidity, then go to dinner, and then prattle all night through to his wife about it: that is living and being interesting.

133.

Order of Precedence in Ethics   1851.

Ethics start out with this demand to every human being, and no nonsense about it: You *must* become perfected; if you are not, it will at once be counted against you. That puts an end to all twaddle about how greatly one wants to do this and that. No, when it comes to the Ethical you can only speak by self-accusation. When you are not becoming perfected, do not, on your life, dare to prattle about how you really would like so much to become a better man, instead you must at once humbly confess: If I am not perfected it is my own fault. *Ethically*, you see, I myself am the only obstacle to my becoming perfected—so it is my own fault. I do want very hard to perfect myself; yes, but to say that something prevents me therefrom is tantamount to libelling God and his Ordinance, it is *lèse-majésté* of the Ethical, it is sly hypocrisy.

134.

Quite Ironical!   *1855.*

There is nothing everyone is so afraid of as of being told how vastly much he is capable of. You are capable of—do you want to know?—you are capable of living in poverty; you are capable of standing almost any kind of maltreatment, abuse, etc. But you do not wish to know about it, isn't that so? You would be furious with him who told you, and only call that person your friend who bolsters you in saying: "No, this I cannot bear, this is beyond my strength, etc."

135.   *1848.*

Actually, a Reformation for the purpose of abolishing the Bible now would have a good deal more validity than Luther's abolition of the Pope. This thing about the Bible has developed religiosity in scholarly and legalistic circles, but merely as entertainment. A sort of "learning" in that field has gradually seeped down to the very lowest class, and no one any longer reads the Bible merely as an individual human being. But this way of reading it causes irreparable harm; it then comes to be a stronghold for apologies and evasions etc. in relation to *living*, for there is constantly some reference one must look up, and always this sham that one must make sure the doctrine is in perfect shape before one can begin to live in accordance with it—which means that one never gets around to it.

The Bible Societies, this insipid caricature of the Missions, a company which, just like any other business-company, works with money, and is busy distributing the Bible in just as worldly a way as other enterprises their wares: the Bible Societies have done irreparable harm. Christianity has long been in need of a religious hero who, in fear and trembling before God, had the courage to forbid people to read the Bible. This is something just as necessary as the necessity of preaching *against* Christianity.

136.   *1843.*

It is quite true what Philosophy says: that Life must be understood backwards. But that makes one forget the other saying: that it must be lived—forwards. The more one ponders this, the more it comes to mean that life in the temporal existence never becomes quite intelligible, precisely because at no moment can I find complete quiet to take the backward-looking position.

137.   *1847.*

There has probably existed many an author more acute and with greater genius than I, but I would like to see one who with keener acumen has reduplicated his very thinking to the second power of dialectics.* It is one thing to be a keen thinker in books, another to reduplicate dialectically one's thinking in his own existence. The former is like a game with no stakes, played merely for the sake of the game, whereas reduplication is like a game the enjoyment of which is intensified by playing for big stakes. Dialectics in books represents only thinking, but reduplication of the thinking means action in life. But a thinker who fails to reduplicate the dialectics of his thinking will constantly develop new illusions. His thinking never receives the final test of action. Only the ethical thinker, by acting, can safeguard himself against communicating illusions.

138.   *1848.*

Reduplication is the core of the Christian teaching. As a doctrine it not only differs from other doctrines, but it is essentially different by being the doctrine that reduplicates and makes the teacher of it important. Questions on Christian matters always must go like this: it is asked not only whether *what* a man says is true from a Christian viewpoint, but: *how* is the man who says it?

So when a man arrayed in silks, with stars and decorations, says that Truth must suffer persecution, etc., then these proportions, this combination, merely produce an esthetic condition. He moves his audience by his presentation—while his appearance assures them that nowadays things surely are not quite that bad—that was in the old days. It is true that this silken man (for he is orthodox; nobody dares deny that) says: "Remember you do not know when the moment may come that you shall suffer for the sake of

Truth," and then the silken man weeps (for he already imagines himself a martyr); but the listener is thinking something like this: "So what!" No, the man's appearance and his whole life tell a different story; he is secure indeed; nowadays Truth is no longer persecuted. Woe upon him!—When, out in the country, in rural peace, some Reverend curses and thunders of a Sunday and is terribly shocked as he sermonizes on how the world persecutes Christians (including his Reverence), it is easy to see that we have here a roguish jester who flatters his own vanity by making believe he is persecuted, while actually he lives in rural security and only frequents peasants and such persons as duly revere him. No, my fine fellow, that too is play-acting. If you want to be in on it in earnest, go to the metropolis and perform on the big stage.

139. 1847.

An artist, a poet, a scientist, etc. may very well go through life generally admired, and it is a matter of chance whether such a man is persecuted or scoffed at. All such persons are in a different category* from the universally human, and their creations do not touch existence essentially, since their medium is the imagination. But a man of Ethics must essentially be persecuted, or else he would be ethically mediocre. An ethical man relates to the universally human (i.e. to each and every human being and in equal degree—there is no distinction), and his relationship to human existence is that of a demand. So if an ethical man finds that people want to admire him (which would be quite right for a poet, an artist, etc., since the relationship is distinct from others), he must himself see that this holds a deception, an untruth. An ethical man must not let people admire him, but—through him—they must be urged toward the Ethical. As soon as people are permitted to admire an ethical man they elevate him into a genius, i.e. put him on a different plane, and, *ethically*, that very thing constitutes the most horrible fallacy, for the ethical shall and must be universally human. An ethical man must constantly maintain, and inculcate in others, that every human being is as capable [of ethical conduct] as he. So there we have a different relationship. Instead of laying claim to admiration (which people are not so very unwilling to give, particularly if it suits their indolence, for instance, by saying: Well, it's easy for him; he is a genius, etc.) he demands *existence* from them: practice what you preach. That makes them angry. They wanted to admire him in order to be rid of him (i.e. the gadfly-sting of his existence) but the human feeling in him that makes him say: anybody can do it as well as I —calls forth hatred and makes people wish to have him at a distance.

And another result of this is that after he is dead they will honor him, as by then the sting inherent in his being their contemporary will have gone. The very objection to such an ethical man during his lifetime becomes a eulogy of him after his death. If the ethical man gives in while he lives, the world will applaud for a moment, but it won't be long before it says that, after all, this showed he was weak—at least the world has that much idea of what it means to be ethical. But if he refuses to give in, it will exasperate the world; yet, after he is dead, that same world will say: He was right, after all.

140.   *1847.*

I work to the limit of my capacity, more and more strenuously, solely devoted to the effort of bringing out my thoughts in their clearest, most beautiful and truest form—heedless of everything else. That is exactly why (because I am disinterested) I am regarded as mad and am slighted. If, like the really great among my contemporaries, I devoted one tenth of my strength to intellectual pursuits and nine tenths to looking after my own interests, saw to it that my bit of work was amply remunerated by money and honors, then I would be a great man, an esteemed and highly respected man!!!

Therefore I dare use without qualms my life as an author as a small example to illustrate the truth, or the truth of the idea which Christianity sets forth (that of the New Testament, not the Sunday-chatter of those clothed in bombazine,* broadcloth, silk and velvet). Oh, young man, be on guard, especially against parsons and poets. Guard against doing what the parson on Sundays calls the Highest (for on Mondays he himself is part of the conspiracy that laughs at you, nay, already Sunday night he will be in his club to learn the latest, to see if anyone has been so crazy as to follow up and do what he told them, so that the Reverend can get something to laugh at, something to deplore as immaturity); guard against doing what the poets praise in verse, for in the humdrum prose of his daily life the poet joins with those who cry *"pereat"*—let him perish—the person who

was stupid enough to . . . etc. Gamble, carouse,
whore, swindle widows and orphans, spread calumny
etc., and the world will forgive you, but above all
guard against the slightest suspicion that you might
take it into your head to realize in your own life
what the parson preaches on Sundays: for then Satan
will be loosed; such a thing can never be forgiven.
It is a life-and-death struggle; everyone who became
a Councilor of Justice, an Excellency, everyone who
in insipid, material security became a hubby and
child-begetter, in brief, to all of these it is of the utmost importance that such an enterprise be strangled
immediately, if possible. Why, a whorer or a gambler
doesn't offend the world, does he? On the contrary, it
pleases the world that there are some who are worse
than the average. But, woe, woe, unto him who,
without saying a word, by his life pokes into the mystery of worldliness! For the world puts up with a
parson preaching on Sunday, because from the parson's life on Monday the congregation easily gathers
how the whole thing is to be interpreted—and one
may as well, to make a good showing, and in order
to mock Our Lord and credulous youths, continue
to adhere to the custom that the lofty virtues are
preached on Sundays by a person who earns his living
in that way. Indeed, if the ordinances regulating Sun-
and-Holy Days were observed consistently, ministers
should be forbidden to preach on Sundays; why favor
one trade above another! When all other shops must
close on Sundays why should the parsons be allowed
to keep theirs open? Actually it is the earning of
money, the turn-over of money, that infringes on the

Blue-Law regulations, since clergymen earn their money on Sundays.

141. *1848.*

Altogether, in relation to Christianity these are the two most outstanding misrepresentations:

1. Christianity is not a doctrine (but then the mischief about orthodoxy cropped up, with quarrels about this and that, while people's lives remained entirely unchanged, and they bickered about what is Christian in the same way as about Platonic philosophy, etc.)—Christianity is a message about existence. That is why each generation must start on it anew; the accumulated erudition of preceding generations is essentially superfluous, yet not to be scorned if it understands itself and its limits, but extremely dangerous if it does not.

2. Christianity not being a doctrine, it is not a matter of indifference, as in the case of a doctrine, *who* expounds it if only (objectively) he says the right thing. No, Christ did not appoint professors, but followers. If Christianity (precisely because it is not a doctrine) is not reduplicated in the life of the person expounding it, then he does not expound Christianity, for Christianity is a message about living and can only be expounded by being realized in men's lives. Altogether, living in it, expressing Christianity in one's life, etc., is what it means to reduplicate.

142. *1848.*

To reduplicate is to be what one professes. Therefore people are infinitely better off with someone who

does not speak too loftily, but *is* what he professes to
be. I have never been bold enough to say that the
world is evil. I make this discrimination: Christianity
teaches that the world is evil. But I dare not say so;
I am far from being pure enough myself for saying
that. But I have said: the world is mediocre, and that
is just what my own life expresses. But how many
milk-sops of parsons stand in their pulpits thunder-
ing about the world being evil—and what, I wonder,
do their lives express?—I have never been bold enough
to say that I would risk everything for the sake of
Christianity. I am not yet that strong. I begin in a
smaller way. I know that I have risked a good deal,
and I think and believe that God will educate me
so that I may learn to risk more. But Mynster weeps
at the thought that he is willing to sacrifice all, as he
says; let all others fall by the wayside, he will stand
pat! God knows what he has risked? One should never
talk like that. The brief kindling of the fire for an
hour on Sundays only leaves one the more sluggish
and slothful afterwards. If one has not yet *done* anything to act, one should never say: I am going to do
it. Instead one may say: Christianity demands it of
me, but since I have not been tested in that way, I
dare not say anything on my account. For instance,
I have been financially independent and therefore
have always spoken with great circumspection about
economic worries, often being reminded that, after
all, I have not experienced them, that I speak like a
poet.

Oh, if only truth prevailed in communication between man and man! One defends Christianity, another attacks Christianity, and when all is said and

done, if one would check their lives, neither one nor the other cares very much about Christianity; it may simply afford them a living.

Now, as far as I am concerned, I have had a thorn in the flesh since my earliest days. If it hadn't been for that, I should probably have progressed far in worldliness by now. But I cannot, no matter how much I might wish to. So I have no merit whatever, for what is meritorious about a person following the right path if he uses a go-cart, or a horse trotting along in the right track when it has a sharp bit in its mouth.

143.   *1850.*

Oh, how true! What Denmark needs is a dead man. At that very instant I shall be victorious as rarely any other human being has been. In that very second all about my spindly legs and my trousers and the nickname "Søren" will be forgotten—no, not forgotten, but interpreted differently, and it will give vast impetus to the cause. In that very second those who shall be my witnesses will speak another language than now, for no renegation will be necessary on their part. Then even my most infinitesimal utterance will acquire significance and find acceptance —while, as it is now, my most gigantic accomplishments are turned away to give room for derision and jealousy.

In the state of moral disintegration, wherein Denmark finds herself today, only the voice of a dead man can break through, a dead man whose whole life was a training aimed at preparing for this very situation: to be able to speak about a dead man.

5. IRONY—THE INDIRECT MODE OF
COMMUNICATION—SOCRATES

144.
*Definition of Irony**   *1846.*

Irony is a combination of ethical passion which in
one's inner forum perpetually accentuates the ego
—and of good breeding which in appearance (in asso-
ciating with people) infinitely abstracts from the ego.
(The latter is the cause that no one notices the former, and therein lies the art upon which the true
infinite perpetuation of the former depends.)

145.   *1846.*

An ironist who sides with the majority is *eo ipso* a
mediocre ironist. To be with the majority is a spontaneous wish of the unreflecting; irony is suspect both
to the right and the left. That is why a true ironist
never belongs to the majority. But the wag does.

146.   *1846.*

That several of Plato's dialogues end without any
concrete result has a far deeper reason than I have
hitherto thought. Indeed Plato emulated Socrates's
maieutic method which incites the listener to independent thinking and therefore does not draw any
conclusion, but leaves a sting. This is an excellent
parody of the modern method of learning by rote,
which brings out everything at once, the sooner the
better, a method that does not arouse any independent mental activity, but only causes the student to
repeat by rote.

147. *1843.*

My destiny seems to be that I shall set forth the truth insofar as I discover it and simultaneously demolish any attendant authority. Then, as I become un-authoritative, and in the highest degree unreliable in the eyes of men, I set forth the truth and thus bring them into a contradiction from which they can only be rescued by absorbing the truth by themselves. Only that personality is mature who absorbs truth and makes it his own, no matter whether it is Bi-leam's ass* talking or a guffawer with his horse-laugh, or an apostle and an angel.

148. *1846.*

People believe, and talk, a lot of rubbish and are moved because Socrates, they think, was so popular. Pshaw, his strolling about talking to cobblers and tanners, etc. was merely ironic polemics against "the learned philosophers"; and then it amused him that it looked as if they were having a conversation (he and the cobbler) since they used the same words; only Socrates used them in an entirely different sense.

149. *1846.*

The art involved in my whole underlying existence consisted not only in abstaining from talking about what occupied me so infinitely and keeping silent about the books in which I gradually laid down my best efforts, but principally in being always at the beck and call of others, ready to talk about every-thing else: jokes, larks, etc., like a man of leisure who has all the time in the world.

150.
What is Popular   *1845.*

One is not unpopular because he uses peculiar expressions; that just so happens; such terms become a fad, and by and by everybody, down to the last simpleton, uses them.

But a person who follows through an idea in his mind is, and always will be, *essentially* unpopular. That was why Socrates was unpopular, though he did not use any special terms, for to grasp and hold *his* "ignorance" requires greater vital effort than understanding the whole of Hegel's philosophy.

151.   *1847.*

Though Socrates is called a popular philosopher *quoad doctrinam,** he is, was and will remain *essentially* unpopular. How many have grasped him, how many live in each generation (and in this respect the accumulation of generations means nothing whatever, for the task must be tackled anew by each individual) who understand that an idea could sway a man to such an extent that for this idea, pursuing this idea, he would go to his death? That is what is meant by heroic, and the heroic too, in essence, will remain equally unpopular in each generation. The heroic has relation to every individual, singly, every individual could become a hero. Heroism has no relation to the difference* between one man and another (genius, artist, poet, noble, etc.) no, heroism means being a virtuoso in "the universally human." Heroism means to be great in what every individual could be great in.

Calling Socrates a genius is very stupid; if he had been a genius he would not have related himself to "the universally human" (i.e. to each human being), but would have placed himself outside it; however, then he would not have been a gadfly.

152.

Why did Socrates compare himself to a gadfly?

1846.

Because he only wished his influence to be ethical. He did not want to be an admired genius, standing apart from the rest, whereby he actually would have made life easier for them, as they would say: "Yes, it's all very fine for him, he is a genius." No, he merely did what every human being can do; he comprehended what every human being can comprehend. Therein lies the epigrammatic. He grabbed hold of the individual and worried him, ceaselessly compelling and teasing him with this ordinary, universally human stuff. That made him a gadfly stirring up a person's passion, and he did not permit that person indolently and effeminately to admire and go on admiring, but claimed his very soul. When a human being possesses ethical strength, people like to elevate him into a genius, just to be rid of him; for his life constitutes a claim, a demand, on them.

153.   *1848.*

It is so that the very power of being superior ends in loss of power. Socrates possessed the power of superiority, that was why he was executed. Had he been like the common herd, he would have whined and

blubbered before the court and flattered the people:
and he would not have been condemned to death. So
it goes with the strong man who can bear every kind
of abuse and meanness easily and smilingly and who,
for that very reason, becomes powerless; if he were
weak, he would command pity and would not have
to suffer at all.

154.   1846.

In my conception, to be victorious does not mean
that *I* triumph, but that the idea triumphs through
me, even though it entails my being sacrificed.

155.

Socrates and the Others   1852.

Socrates always kept talking merely about food and
drink—but in reality he was constantly talking and
thinking about the Infinite.

The others constantly talked in the loftiest tones
about the Infinite; in reality they were constantly
talking and thinking about food and drink, money
and profit.

156.

The Existential—Rhetorics (Eloquence)   1851.

The greater effort a man puts into his daily living,
the more disinclined he becomes to making speeches.
Cf. Socrates. Such a man understands only too well
that all the splendid speech-making and masterly
oratory lead people, not into, but away from, the
Existential, which daily goes on presenting its petty
problems, but does not come up with brilliant situ-
ations and fascinating matters. Therefore such a man
will say: Goodness me, what would it amount to if I

took an hour's declamation once a week or once a year!—No, instead, such a man becomes an ironist, a teaser. What does that mean? That means that all along he juxtaposes life's trivia with the highest, calls attention to the fact that while, in one sense there is question of the loftiest matters, the rub is that it is also a matter of the most humdrum trifles; in brief he does not esthetically place problems at a distance.

On the other hand, the less a person lives a personal life, the greater his urge for rhetorical effusions.

Now, reflect on the state of affairs in Christendom.

157.

A Socrates in Christendom   *1850.*

Socrates could not prove that the soul was immortal. He merely said: This matter occupies me so much that I will order my life as though immortality were a fact—should it prove to be wrong, *eh bien*, then I won't regret my choice; for this is the only matter I am concerned about.

What a great help it would be already in Christendom if someone said, and acted accordingly: I don't know if Christianity is true, but I will order my whole life as if it were, stake my life thereon—then if it proves not to be true, *eh bien*, I don't regret my choice, for it is the only matter I am concerned about.

158.

Socrates—Christianity   *1854.*

Socrates is right: if a man does not do right, it is because he does not understand it; if he understood, he would do what is right—*ergo*: sin is ignorance.

Christianity is right: sin is guilt. For when a man does not do right, it is quite rightly because he does not understand it; if he understood, etc. But the reason he does not understand what is right, is that he cannot understand it, and that he cannot understand it is because he *will* not understand it—so there is the rub.

And only by treating EVERYTHING as criminal has Christianity been able to manage the world and has managed to keep order.

159.   *1846.*

What ability there is in an individual may be measured by the yardstick of how far there is between his *understanding* and his *will*. What a person can understand he must also be able to force himself to *will*. Between understanding and willing is where excuses and evasions have their being.

160.   *1846.*

If a person does not become what he understands, he does not really understand it. Only Themistocles* understood Miltiades; therefore he became what he became.

161.

Contrasting Images   *1853.*

Bernard of Clairvaux is preaching a crusade under the open sky (*cf.* the passage in Böhringer); thousands upon thousands are gathered; he has not even time to finish before a thunderous cry goes up from the

crowd: The Cross, the Cross!—that, you see, is working in the direction of man's brute destiny kneading
human beings into a herd.

Oh Socrates, Thou Noble Sage! Amid the crowd,
surrounded by these thousands upon thousands, thou
workest to split up "the herd" and seek out "the individual" that represents man's spiritual destiny. And
Bernard was a Christian, and it was in Christendom
it happened—and Socrates was a pagan—and yet there
is more Christianity in the Socratic method than in
the method of Saint Bernard.

162.

Christianity's Confusion   *1853.*

Christianity means: practice what you preach; a char-
acter-task.

Making Christianity into a doctrine, an object for
inactive, brooding meditation has resulted in that
baleful species of thinkers who will fill 40 pages with
their imaginings and then end on p. 41 by saying
that, when all is said and done, it is impossible to
comprehend the matter fully. Oh, what woeful waste
of time. And even St. Augustine was like that!

How clear, how virginally pure, if I so may say, is
not Socrates *qua* thinker, with his energetic distinction between what he grasps and comprehends and
what he doesn't! If on p. 41 one must read that, when
all is said and done, it is still impossible to comprehend it, then it would be Socratic to save the preceding 40 pages. However, if this method were
adopted what would happen to all the professors?

163.

Irony   *1854.*

Basically my whole existence is the deepest irony.

Going to South America, descending into subterranean caverns to dig up remains of vanished animal-
forms and antediluvian fossils: there is nothing ironical about that, for the animals one comes across today
living in such places do not, after all, pretend to be
the same as the ancient ones.

But plumb in the middle of "Christendom" to want
to excavate the foundation of what it means to be a
Christian, which bears almost the same relation to
our contemporary Christians as the bones of the ancient animals to those now living: that is the most
intense irony. The irony is that while Christianity is
supposed to exist there are at the same time thousands of prelates in velvet, silks and broadcloth, millions of Christians begetting Christians etc.

What did Socrates's irony actually consist of? Could
it be certain terms and turns of speech or such? No,
these are mere trifles; maybe virtuosity in speaking
ironically? Such things do not constitute a Socrates.
No, his entire life was irony and consisted of this:
while the whole contemporary population of farm-
stewards and tradespeople etc., in brief, these thousands, while all of them were absolutely sure that
they were human beings and knew what it meant to
be a human being, Socrates probed in depth (ironically) and busied himself with the problem: *what
does it mean to be a human being?* By so doing he
really expressed that all the *treiben* [bustle] of these

thousands was an illusion, a phantasmagoria, a tumult, a noise, a bustle, etc. which, from the viewpoint of idea equals zero, or less than zero, in so far as these people could apply their lives to try to find out about ideality.

The irony in relation to Christianity contains another element besides the Socratic, insofar as people in Christendom not only imagine themselves to be human beings (here of course Socrates halts) but also imagine themselves to be that historically concrete thing which being a Christian represents. Socrates doubted that a person was a human being at birth; it doesn't come so easy, and neither does the knowledge of what it means to be a human being, for it was the ideality of man that occupied Socrates; that was what he was looking for. But what, one wonders, would Socrates think if he were told that human beings have long since become so perfectible and have made such progress in nonsense that now there is good sense in a child almost being *born* a Christian, nay, being born into a "distinct denomination."

6. TOWARD THE CATASTROPHE

164.   *1847.*

That girl has caused me enough trouble. Now she is —not dead—but well and happily married.* On that day (6 years ago) I said that would happen, and was declared to be the most abject of all abject scoundrels. Very peculiar!

165.
NB-NB.

Wednesday April 19, 1848.

My whole being has changed. My secretiveness and
reserve are broken—I must speak out.

Great God, Grant me Mercy!

My father really spoke the truth when he said: "You
will never amount to anything as long as you have
money." He spoke prophetically; he believed I would
go in for carousing and revelry. But that wasn't
exactly it. No, but I—with my keen mind and my
melancholy, and money to boot: oh, what favorable
conditions for developing all the torments of self-
torture in my heart!

(Strangely *à propos*, just as I had resolved to speak
out my doctor came. However, I did not speak then,
it would have been too sudden for me. But my resolve
is firm: I will speak out.

Maundy-Thursday and Good Friday have become
true Holy Days for me.)

166.   *1848.*

Alas, she could not break the silence of my melancholy. That I loved her—nothing is more certain—and
thus my melancholy was given more than enough to
feed on, oh, it received something horrible in addition.† That I became a writer is essentially owing to
her, my melancholy, and my money. Now, with God's
help, I shall become my real self, I have faith that
Christ will help me overcome my melancholy, and
that I will become a minister.

In my melancholy I still loved the world, for I

loved my melancholy. Everything has concurred to make the relationship more tense: her sufferings, all my efforts, and finally that I have been an object of ridicule; all this, with God's help has contributed to my finally breaking through, now that I am reduced to the necessity of earning my livelihood.

† And yet she could not have become mine. I was and still am a penitent and only had my penalty terribly increased by having started that relationship.

167.

NB-NB.

Easter Monday   *April 24, 1848.*

No, no, my reserve cannot be broken after all, at least not now. The idea of wanting to break it will come to occupy me so much and in such a way at every moment that this reserve will only become more firmly entrenched.

Still, it is a comfort to have spoken to my doctor. I have often gone about in fear of myself: that I might perhaps be too proud to confide in anyone. But as I have done it before, so I have done it again now. And what can my doctor actually tell me? Nothing. But it is important for me that I have respected the competent human tribunal.

My intellectual activity satisfies me so completely and will make me accept everything joyfully, if only I may go on devoting myself to it. So I can also see my life like this: that I announce to others the good tidings of comfort and gladness, while I myself remain bound in pain of which I can anticipate no alleviation—except this one thing: that I may carry on my work of mind and spirit. Oh, in that respect I certainly have no objection to raise against my life-condition; on the contrary, I thank God every day for having vouchsafed me much more than I ever expected, I pray to Him every day that He will suffer me to give thanks to Him—He knows that.

But the matter was this. My future was becoming more and more of a problem in regard to my liveli-hood. Now, if I were not saddled with this hampering reserve I could become a state official. Now that is difficult. Then for a long time I brooded on whether, after all, it would not be possible for me to break through, and because hitherto I have essentially oper-ated by evasion, as an escapist, I have often thought it was my duty (especially since my reserve may become a cause for sin in me) to make an attempt at taking the offensive.

If I hadn't done so, I would always have reproached myself. Now I have done it and understand myself again, better than before, wherein precisely this has helped me.

I now put my hope in God, praying that in some way or other He will aid my activity as a writer or add to my livelihood in some other way, and thus permit me to go on with my writing.

It is true that I believe in forgiveness for our sins, but I understand it in this way: that I must bear my penalty as heretofore, which means that I must re-main in the painful prison of my reserve to the end of my days, remote, in a deeper sense, from commu-nity with others—yet feeling my penalty attenuated by the thought that God has forgiven me. I cannot, at least not yet, rise so high in faith (such frankly trusting faith I cannot yet win) that I can eliminate this painful memory by faith. But clinging to faith I ward off despair, bear the pain and penalty of my reserve—and am so indescribably happy or blissful in that activity of mind and spirit which God so plentifully and mercifully has vouchsafed me.

If my reserve were to be broken it might perhaps rather occur by God somehow helping me to a permanent position, and maybe He is now helping me to turn my mind in that direction. But wanting to dislodge my reserve in this formal manner by ceaselessly thinking about it is bound to lead to the opposite result.

168. *1848.*

If I dared make up with her *that* would be my only wish and would give me deep inward joy. But I bear the responsibility for her marriage [to Schlegel]. If she learned from me with certainty how she has been and still is loved, she would regret her marriage. What holds her to it is the thought that, no matter how much she saw in me, admired me and loved me, I still acted shabbily toward her. She has not had enough religious faith to face it out alone with an unhappy infatuation—I never have dared to help her directly; it has cost me enough suffering.

If I hadn't also felt bliss in melancholy and sadness I couldn't possibly have lived without her. On those days—few and far between—when I was really humanly happy I always longed for her indescribably, this girl whom I had loved so much and who, moreover, had touched me so deeply by her pleading. But

my melancholy and the sufferings of my soul are the
reasons why, humanly speaking, I have always been
unhappy—wherefore I would have had no happiness
to share with her. However, I dare not write down
anything about her—as long as I live I bear the responsibility for her future.

169.   1848.

All this fear of Germany is imagination, a game, a
new attempt to flatter the national vanity. One million people who fairly and honestly admitted to
themselves that they were a small nation and, before
God, resolved, each on his own account, to be just
that, constitute a huge power; here there is no danger. No, the misfortune is something else; the misfortune is that this small nation is demoralized,
divided against itself, each man disgustingly envious
of his neighbor, recalcitrant to anyone in authority,
petty-minded with anybody who is "somebody,"
brazen and unbridled, stirred and dredged up to a
kind of tyranny of the populace. That gives a bad
conscience, and that is why the Germans are feared.
But no one dares say openly what is the true cause of
the misfortune, and so all these unhealthy passions
are flattered and the people acquire self-importance
by standing up to the Germans.

Denmark is facing a nasty period. Small-town spirit
and petty grouching keep up mutual bickering;
finally it will be so that a person is suspected of being
German if he does not wear a certain kind of hat, etc.,
etc. On the other side there is the communist rebellion;* anyone with a little property is pilloried and
persecuted in the press.

That is how Denmark's misfortune looks—or it is Denmark's punishment, a nation not truly god-fearing, a nation whose national conscience is on the level of town-gossip, a nation that worships the idea of being Nothing, a nation where schoolboys are judges, where those who should rule are afraid, and those who should obey are bold as brass, a nation where one can daily see new evidence of the fact that there is no public morality in the land—a nation that must be saved either by a tyrant, or by a few martyrs.

170.   *1848.*

But I need physical recreation and rest. Reading the proofs of my last book* at such a time; my misgivings as to its publication; the financial situation in these difficult times; seven years of continuous work; that I must move to another apartment; that they even take away my Anders*; and I am all alone—yet constantly (God be praised! the only thing that helps me) writing and producing (for even these last days I have been working on my new book about the Sickness unto Death):* all this has strained me a little. Also, this year I had counted on traveling—a lot even —but now there is no place one can travel to.

Hence some troubled doubt—which yet with God's help shall aid me, and has aided me, to understand myself better. Praise be to God; this is still the sunny side of my life, this, God be praised, hitherto inexhaustible fountain of joy that always renews itself: that God is Love.

I understand more and more that Christianity actually has too much bliss to offer us humans. Just think what it means to dare believe that God came

into the world also for my sake. It almost sounds like
the most blasphemous, arrogant presumption that a
human being should dare to believe such a thing. If
it were not that God himself had said it—if man had
invented it to show how significant a human being is
to God: then, indeed, of all blasphemies this would
be the most horrible. That is why it was not invented
to show how significant a human being is to God,
but to show what an infinite love is God's love. For
indeed it is infinite love that he cares for a sparrow,
but that he let himself be born and died for the sake
of sinners (and a sinner is even less than a sparrow):
oh, infinite love!

171.   *1848.*

I hardly think I have many years left to live, but
whether I have one hour or seventy years, my choice
is made: every moment (insofar as I may be able to
spare some time for recreation, but for that I shall
ask God's permission) I will use to set forth Christianity. It is only too true that (in the main) Christianity has been abolished. And in that respect I am
like a spy.

172.   *1848.*

There isn't a human being I reproach with anything;
they have not understood me. Even at this moment
I cannot let go of the thought which I have had from
the very beginning, whether after all every person
does not, deep down, think of God. I have never
overlooked anyone, not the simplest servant-lad or
maid—alas, for he who is "for God" must instantly
shudder in his deepest soul at the thought: suppose

God in turn should overlook you. This is and will remain my misfortune: humanly speaking I have done
far too much for people. I may have pretended to
overlook them—alas, precisely because I hardly dared
admit how much they were on my mind—so that I
shouldn't be considered completely crazy.

Merely having neglected to say good-day to a serv-
ant-girl was enough to upset me as though I had
committed a crime, as though God would have to
give me up.—And withal I am persecuted for my
arrogance!

In everything I have seen a relationship of Duty
involving God, but nobody seems to have had any
duty to me.

173. *1848.*

The issue is neither more nor less than a revision of
Christianity, it is a matter of eliminating 1800 years
as though they never had been. That I shall succeed
therein I believe fully and firmly; all is clear as day
to me. Yet I feel more and more acutely that at the
least impatience, the least wilfulness, I am halted,
my thoughts grow confused.

I rise in the morning and thank God—and then I
start my work. At a set hour in the evening I stop,
and I thank God—and then I go to sleep. And so I
live, though not, at certain moments, without fits of
melancholy and sadness, yet, in the main, day in and
day out in the most blissful enchantment. Alas, so
I live in Copenhagen, and in Copenhagen I am the
only person not considered serious, the only person
who is useless and who does not accomplish anything,
a half-crazy original. That is the way the crowd judges

me, and the few who see a little deeper really do not object to this becoming the general judgment about me.

174.
The past summer   *1849.*

seems to have been intended to support me in what, after all, I have understood to be my task: to stop my creative writing now; it has been a painful summer constantly confronting me with some new outside worry, as soon as an old one was done with.

The war has deprived me of Anders; the impression I felt of my home grew dim, and the extremely bad turn in Strube's* illness further dimmed it; and I wished I were far away, but it was impossible for me to leave.

Add to this all my economic worries together with the fatal blow that, before we know a word of it, we shall probably be saddled with an income tax.*

Then Reitzel* too has been enough to drive me to despair. When being a writer involves such sacrifices as I have had to make, then to lose money now *qua* writer, and maybe through my pamphlet mar my future, is bad enough; then not even to have a compliant publisher but one who plagues me with his fears and misgivings and his unreasonable request to let him print 1 or 2 quires a week and issue the book at a more convenient time of year! All of that came to naught, it is true, but it is excruciating in my circumstances to experience things like that.

Furthermore, the tanner from whom I rent my apartment, has tormented me with stench all summer long. Many, many a time I have had to use mental power, as it were, to avoid becoming sick with impatience. Maltreated as I was in many ways by vulgarity and prying curiosity, my home used to be a consolation to me; having a pleasant home was my greatest earthly encouragement. That was why I rented so excellent and so expensive an apartment —and then to pay 200 rixdollars to suffer like that!

Then again and again I have been assailed by doubts as to the publication of my finished products.

Enjoying any entertainment has been made almost impossible for me in Copenhagen because, the moment I appear, the public directs a baneful curiosity on my person.

With all that I also have suffered the usual discomfort that summer brings me.

Then State Councilor Olsen died, and that brought me new worries.

And during all this I have had to deny myself my essential mainstay: I have not dared start on any new work, let alone impart speed and impetus to it. Once I decided to stop writing. Yet writing is my true life.

Of course my melancholy has gained in scope, which would not have happened otherwise; for in creative writing I lose myself completely.

In truth, it has been a hard time for me. I can only interpret it as a discipline in patience, and hope that thus it will benefit me truly. No matter how painful, it must help me to become more concrete.

But let me never forget to thank God for the indescribable Good he has vouchsafed me, far more than I ever expected. And may it always remain true for me what originally was in my soul, that blessed thing: God is Love, His wisdom infinite, and His possibilities infinite, whereas I merely have the intelligence of a sparrow, and where I scarcely can count on one possibility, He has millions of possibilities.

175.

NB.   *1849.*

No, no, I cannot;* also it seems impossible that I should now be able to soar higher and more boldly than when I was favored by having independent means. No, no, when they are gone I must secure my existence by some official appointment or in some other way—as I have always imagined that I would have to do—I cannot go beyond that; it would be tantamount to tempting God.

All that I have entered in my Journal under NB¹⁰* about myself is absolutely true. I need favored treatment in order to soar above myself ruthlessly. Essentially I am a poet, a genius. I am not one to direct and rule everything; that is not my intention, but though tied and bound I am being used by the hand of a higher Power through my melancholy and my consciousness of sin. I myself am like reflection incarnate:* always in reverse. (It is against my self-denial to admit my activity openly.*) That is why I have shuddered again and again, and despite all my religious strivings I still shudder, at the idea of appearing in the role of author in conditions that somehow would obligate me for a prolonged period, maybe for my whole lifetime, on a definite scale, and that precisely at the moment when I am about to train myself to put on mourning for my deteriorating economic situation.

176.   *1849*.

The other thing* may be foolhardier, may be bolder, may perhaps involve more daring and risk, but that does not make it more true to my inner self—and after all, being true to that comes first.

If I consider my personal life, am I really a Christian? Or is this personal existence of mine not purely a poet's existence, maybe even with a dash of something demoniacal* added? The idea would then be to *dare* on such a vast scale that I might make myself so unhappy that I would thus have prepared the ground for becoming a true Christian. But even so, am I allowed to make it dramatic, to involve a whole country's Christianity in the game? Is there not something desperate in all this: by treachery, as it were, committing arson in order to throw oneself into God's arms? Perhaps there is, for perhaps it would turn out that I had not become a Christian.

However, all this about my author's personality cannot be used, for it is obvious that it will make me sink deeper into "the Interesting" instead of climbing out of it, and that is exactly how my contemporaries will judge it. The simple transition must be made simply by my keeping silent and trying to obtain some official appointment.

If that came about, it is absolutely certain that I should stop being an author, still I would like to take this much of "the Interesting" along: that I myself had put a stop to it and thus officially remained in character. The simple thing to do is quietly and silently to change over to the New, and this solemn wanting to put a full-stop to a period is an extremely dangerous affair; the simple thing is that a full-stop be, in fact, effectively put.

I must regret, and accuse myself, that in a good many of the entries in this Journal there are attempts at exalting my own self, which I beg God to forgive me.

Up to now I have been a writer, definitely nothing more, and it means a desperate struggle for me to wish to pass beyond my confines.

Though it is true that the pamphlet "*Training in Christianity*" has great personal significance for me, does it follow that I must publish it immediately here and now? Maybe I am one of the few who need very strong remedies: should I then, instead of benefiting from my own medicine and beginning in real earnest to become a Christian, publish it first? A phantastic idea.

This pamphlet and the other pamphlets are written; they exist; and maybe a time will come when they will be propitious, and I shall find the strength to issue them, and that by then they will have become inner truth for me.

It is true in many ways that all my creative writing constitutes my education—all right, does that then mean that instead of, in earnest, becoming a true Christian, I shall now become a phenomenon in the world?

Ergo: Now *The Sickness unto Death* will be published, but pseudonymously with me as editor. I call it "for edification"; that is higher than my category, the writer-category: "edifying."

Like the river Guadalquivir (this image has occurred to me before and will be found somewhere in the Journal) which at a certain point rushes underground, so also there is a stretch: "the edifying," that bears my name. There is something else that is lower (the Esthetic) which is pseudonymous, because my personality does not correspond to it.

The pseudonym I use is: Johannes Anticlimacus, in contrast to Climacus who proclaimed himself a Non-Christian; Anticlimacus is at the opposite pole, he being a Christian to an extraordinary degree—if only I myself could manage quite simply to become a Christian!

"Training in Christianity" can be published in the same way, but there is no hurry.

But nothing that concerns my person as an author [must be published]; it would constitute the untruth of wanting to anticipate, while still alive, which merely amounts to turning oneself into something "Interesting."*

Altogether, henceforth it is in quite different directions I am to be daring. I shall dare to believe that by Christ's help I can be saved from the grip of the melancholy in which I have been living; and I shall dare to try being more economical.

177.
*De se ipso**   *1849.*

Actually something different from what I originally planned will happen.

When I started out as author of *Either-Or* I believe I had a far deeper impression of Christianity's *"awful terror"* than any prelate in the land. I felt fear and trembling as maybe none other. Not that it prompted me to give up Christianity. No. I explained it to myself in a different way. For one thing, as you know, I had learned at an early age that there are human beings destined, as it were, to suffer; secondly, I was conscious of having sinned gravely, therefore I thought Christianity must come to me in the guise of this awful terror. But how cruel and fallacious of me, I thought, if on that account I should terrify others, perhaps disturb many, many happy lovable lives about which it might very well be true that they are genuine Christians. It was utterly alien to my nature to want to terrify others, on the contrary; pathetically, and perhaps also a little proudly, I found my joy in consoling others and in being to them the very soul of gentleness—concealing the terrifying things in my inmost depths.

So my intention was, in a humorous form (to make easy reading) to give my contemporaries a hint, in case they didn't spontaneously realize that greater pressure was needed—but I would stop at that; my heavy pack I intended to keep to myself as my cross. I often have disapproved when a person who, in the strictest sense, was a sinner immediately would get busy terrifying others.—Here lies the burden of my *Concluding Postscript.**

Then I saw, appalled, what a Christian state could be like (I saw it particularly in 1848); I saw that those whose task it was to rule both in the Church and in the State hid like cowards, while abject meanness was brazenly rampant, and I found out how such a Christian state rewards truly god-fearing and truly unselfish endeavor (that is, my endeavor as a writer).

That decided my fate. It is now up to our contemporary age to make up its mind as to what price-tag, what quotation, it wants to put on being Christian; how appalling. I shall probably—I almost said 'unfortunately'—be vouchsafed strength for that. In truth, I do not say it boastfully. I both have been and am now more than willing to pray God to spare me this appalling business; besides I am a human being myself, and I too love, humanly speaking, to be happy here below. But if what one sees nowadays throughout Europe, if that is supposed to be Christianity, Christian states, then I intend to make a start here in Denmark: quote the price of being a Christian that will make the whole conception: State-Church, Clergy as Officials, Livings—explode.

I dare not act otherwise, for I am a penitent of whom God may demand all. But my pseudonymous state is also due to my being a penitent. In any case I shall continue to be an object of persecution, whereas I am guaranteed not to receive any honor or esteem that might be forthcoming from other parts.

Already for some years now I have been accustomed to bear a small country's treachery and ingratitude, the envy of people of status and the scoffing of the rabble, so that—for lack of a better man—I may be fit to preach Christianity. Let Bishop Mynster then keep his velvet canonicals and his Order of the Grand Cross.

178.
My Life's Course   *1852*.

Suffering terrible inner torment I became a writer. Then year after year I went on being a writer and suffered for the sake of the Idea, in addition to which I bore my inner sufferings.

Then 1848 came. That helped. There came a moment when, blissfully overwhelmed, I dared say to myself: I have comprehended the Highest. In truth, such a thing is not vouchsafed to many in each generation.

But almost in the same instant something new came crashing down on me: the Highest, after all, is not to *comprehend* the Highest, but to do it.

It is true that I had been aware of this from the very start; that is why I am something else again than an author in the ordinary sense of the word. On the other hand, I did not realize so clearly that by having private means and being independent it was easier for me to express existentially the thing I had comprehended.

Then when I had understood *that*, I was willing to stand forth as a writer, since having private means made action easier for me than for other writers.

But here it is again: the Highest is *not* to *comprehend* the Highest, but *to do it*, and note this well, including all the burdens it involves.

Only then did I properly understand that "Mercy" must find a place in the plan; if not, a human being would suffocate the moment he was about to start.

But, but—"Mercy" should not be included in order to prevent effort, so here it is again: the Highest is not to comprehend the Highest, but to do it.

VI

CHRISTIANITY

1. THE TASK

179.

My Task   *1854.*

is new in this sense that in the 1800th year of Christianity there is literally no one from whom I can learn how to go about it.

For hitherto all who were above the ordinary have been active in the direction of spreading Christianity, but my task lies in the direction of halting its mendacious spreading and also, I suppose, in the direction of making Christianity shake off a lot of Christians who are so in name only.

Therefore, literally none of the men above the ordinary has been as solitary as I—let alone realized, that one of their tasks was to defend their solitude and guard it—for if a halt must be called, it is easy to see that the less personnel used for it, the better for the solution of the task.

Well, thank you! When I am dead there will be something for the university lecturers to poke into. The abject scoundrels! And yet, what's the use, what's the use? Even though this be printed and read again and again, the lecturers will still make a profit out of me, teach about me, maybe adding a comment like this: "The peculiar thing about this is that it cannot be taught."

180.   *1854*.

How far Christianity is from being a living reality may best be seen in me.

For even with my clear knowledge of it I am still not a Christian. Yet I still cannot help feeling that despite the abyss of nonsense in which we are stuck, we shall all of us be saved. This is the result of my having been fed a directly opposite brand of Christianity as a child.

However, my position is sufficiently difficult. I am not a heathen to whom an apostle, briefly and pithily, expounds Christianity; no, I am a man who, so to speak, must discover Christianity by himself, dig down to make it emerge from the perverted state it has sunk to.

181.   *1849*.

They have changed Christianity and have made it too much of a *consolation*, and forgotten that it is a *demand* upon man. Woe unto the lax preachers! As a result it will be that much harder for him who must preach Christianity anew.

2. WHAT IS CHRISTIANITY?

182.   *1848*.

Well, the real conflict between Christianity and man lies in that Christianity is *Absolute*, or teaches that there exists something Absolute, and demands of the Christian that his life must express the existence of something Absolute. It is *in this sense* that I say I have never known a Christian; I have never seen anyone whose life expressed *that*. People's Christianity consists of profession upon profession, assertions of orthodoxy, attacks on heterodoxy, etc., but their lives, exactly like those of the heathens, reveal that man exists in relativity. People's lives are nothing but relativities.

183.

NB. NB.   *1848.*

Being a Christian holds a double danger.

First, all the inner sufferings involved in becoming a Christian, the fact of giving up reason and becoming crucified to a paradox. This is what my *Concluding Postscript* is about, presenting the matter as ideally as possible.

Then there is the danger facing the Christian who must live in the world of worldliness and demonstrate that he is a Christian. That is what all my later production is about, and it will culminate in what I have ready on my desk now, which could be published under the title: *The Collected Works on Consummation.**

Then when this is done, the question will burst forth with elementary force, as it were: but how on earth does it occur to a person to subject himself to all this; why must he be a Christian when it is so hard? The answer to this might be, in the first place: Shut up! Christianity is the Absolute, a Must. But there could also be another answer: Because the consciousness of sin within him will not leave him in peace, the pain of it fortifies him to bear everything else, if only he can find redemption.

This means that the pain of sin must be very deep in a human being; therefore it must be presented as it is, *so* difficult that it becomes truly obvious that Christianity is only related to the consciousness of sin. Any attempt to become a Christian for any other reason is quite literally lunacy; and that is how it should be.

184.

Life's Worth   1854.

Not until a man has become so utterly unhappy, or has grasped the woefulness of life so deeply that he is moved to say, and mean it: life for me has no value —not till then is he able to make a bid for Christianity.

And then his life may acquire the very highest value.

185.   1848.

The point about Christianity is that it is right around us. That is why no poet, no orator, can paint it, for they use too much imagination. Precisely on that account (that is, for the wrong reason) people love and esteem poets and orators. For *at a distance* men see Christianity as a lovable thing.

Only a dialectician can represent it, as he constantly eliminates all delusions, drilling it, as it were, into our present existence right here. That is why such a dialectician will be ill liked, for *at close range* Christianity is hateful and shocking.

186. *1849.*

Basically, many people think that the Christian commandments (as for instance: Love thy neighbor as thyself) intentionally are made rather too strict—almost like the clock by which a household rises and which is put half an hour fast to prevent the members from getting up too late.

187.

Christian piety—Jewish piety *1851.*

I must admit that I have never seen a Christian in the strict sense of the word. Among the so-called Christians I have seen some fine specimens of Jewish piety.

Jewish piety rests on the idea: Keep close to God, and things will go well with you, the closer you keep to Him the better; and, in any case, you always have God to hold on to.

Christianity expresses something entirely different: the closer you keep to God, and the more involved you get with Him, the worse for you. It is almost as if God said to man: You had better go over to "Tivoli" [an amusement park in Copenhagen] and have a good time with the rest—but whatever you do, don't get yourself involved with me, for that will only bring you misery, humanly speaking.

And not only that: in the end God also abandons the Christian, as shown by the example of the model [Christ].

For, in a strict sense, being a Christian means: to die to the world—and then to be sacrificed; first a sword pierces the heart (to die from the world), and then to be hated, cursed by men and abandoned by God (i.e. sacrificed).

In other words, Christianity is superhuman. And yet the New Testament bids the Christian take up the imitation of Christ.

I am not able to do that. I can only get so far as to use the "model" for humiliation, not for imitation, and once again for humiliation, for it is humiliating that I cannot use the "model" in any other way.

188.   *1849.*

Initially, and principally, Christianity is and must be so terrifying that only an absolute *Must* can drive a person to it. But this initial principle has been abolished, and thereupon came the adoption of the second step of Christianity: meek gentleness, and that is what—for various reasons—is now recommended; one defends it, etc.

But it will cost our generation dearly. For like a spoiled child who, to its own detriment, manages to wheedle its parents into not being strict, so our generation, to its own detriment, has managed to fool or frighten those who should command and wield authority, into not daring to say: Thou shalt!

What the world needs most of all today is this "Thou shalt" uttered with authority. That alone can set things going, and he who would implore another: "Speak severely to me," might not have a bad sense of his own weal.

"Thou shalt" is abolished, however. In every relationship, even in Sunday sermons, our contemporaries are appealed to as if *they* constituted a final court of appeal;* the orator and the grocer recommend their respective cause and wares, be it Christianity or raisins. But there is no teacher anywhere, and no gathering of men being taught, oh, far from it: every gathering is the master, and the individual has to pass his examination under that master.

189.

On Forgiveness of Sin   *1848.*

Believing that his sins have been forgiven is the decisive crisis through which a human being becomes spirit; he who does not believe that is not spirit. It constitutes spiritual maturity; it means that all spontaneity* has been lost, that man not only cannot do anything of himself, but can only do harm to himself. But how many experience in actual truth, quite personally, the understanding of themselves that they have been brought to such an extremity. (Here lies the Absurd. The scandal. The paradox. The forgiveness of sin.)

Most human beings never become mind-and-spirit;* they never have that experience. The development they undergo from childhood, youth, manhood, to old age: don't praise them for that; it is not their "*Zuthat*," their merit, it is a vegetative or an animal-vegetative process. But they never experience any spiritual development.

You see, forgiveness of sin does not concern a special thing, as if one were totally good (that is the childlike idea, for the child always asks forgiveness for some particular thing: that yesterday it did so, today it forgot so and so, etc.; it never would occur to a child, he couldn't even get it into his head, that it is

evil); no, forgiveness of sin does not apply so much to
the particular as to the general; it concerns one's
whole self which is sinful and has a corrupting effect
as soon as it gets the least bit of leeway.

He who then in truth has experienced, and experiences, the belief that his sins have been forgiven
probably becomes a changed man. Everything is forgotten—yet it is not with him as with the child who,
after having been forgiven, remains essentially unchanged. No, a man has added an eternity to his age;
for now he has become spirit, all spontaneity and
attendant selfishness, its selfish clinging to the world
and to its own self, are lost. Now, humanly speaking,
he is old, extremely old, but from the viewpoint of
eternity he is young.

190.

On Forgiveness of Sin   1848.

Psychologically, the problem here lies in a totally different direction than is generally imagined.

The difficulty is: to what kind of spontaneity* the
person reverts who believes it, or what kind of spontaneity follows upon this belief, how is it related to
what one generally calls spontaneity?

To believe in forgiveness of sin is a paradox, is an
absurdity, etc. etc.; that is not what I am talking
about, but something else.

I assume then that someone has had the extreme
courage of faith to believe, in truth, that God literally has forgotten his sins—a courage not found maybe
in ten persons in each generation, this insane courage: after having developed a reasoned idea of God
then to believe that God quite literally can forget.

Still, I assume it. Then what? So all is forgotten
now; the forgiven one is like a new man. But does it
not leave any trace at all, that is, would it be possible that such a person could start all over again and
live a carefree youth? Impossible!

And precisely from this I draw the proof that it is
indescribably injudicious to raise a child strictly in
Christianity, as that merely serves to confuse its life
on the most horrible scale until it has become a man
somewhere in his early thirties.

How would it be possible that a man who really
believed that his sins were forgiven could become
young enough to fall in love erotically?

There lies the problem of my own life. A very old
man raised me extremely strictly in Christianity, and
that is why I feel my life to be so terribly confused,
that is why I have been brought into collisions which
nobody thinks, let alone talks, about. And not until
now, in my thirty-fifth year, may I have learned—by
dint of heavy suffering and with the bitterness of
repentance—to die to the world to the extent that I
might truly find my life and my salvation in a belief
centering on forgiveness of sin. But, in sooth, though
spiritually strong as never before, I am by now far too
old to fall in love with a woman, etc.

A certain exhausted decrepitude is required to feel
a real need for Christianity. If it is forced upon one
earlier it makes for madness. There is in the child
and the youth something that is such a natural,
integral part of their natures that it could be said
God willed them to be so; the child and the youth
are essentially in the category of the "psyche," neither
more nor less. Christianity is spirit. To conceive of a

child as being strictly in the category of "spirit" is a cruelty comparable to killing it, and this Christianity never intended.

Because children are raised in it, Christianity throughout Christendom has mainly become chit-chat. For it is very, very seldom that a child is raised in it with the utmost severity which still, if the worse comes to the worst, is much to be preferred, even though it kills his childhood and youth; as a rule, Christianity is taught in a merely trivial way, and that is absolutely no good. However you look at it, it is better to have borne all these torments in one's childhood and youth by being racked (as someone undergoing torture) on the category of "spirit," which one has not yet attained, to have stood all these torments that made one's childhood an utter misery— and then at long last, fully saved, understand that *now* I can use Christianity, now it exists for me and is my All: *this*, after all, is better than trivially having been neither one thing nor the other.

191.

How was it possible that Jesus Christ could be crucified?   *1847.*

Once upon a time there was a man, whose parents had inculcated in him a pious belief in Jesus Christ— as he grew older he understood it less and less. "For," said he, "I do understand that He was willing to sacrifice His life for Truth and that, when He did sacrifice His life, it was for the sake of Truth. But what I cannot understand is that He who is love did not, because of His love for humanity, prevent men from committing the biggest of all crimes, that of killing Him."

The thing is: Christ is not love, least of all in the human meaning; He is *Truth,* Absolute Truth; therefore He not only could defend their action, but He *had* to let men become guilty of his death: i.e. reveal Truth to the uttermost degree (the contrary, being weakness, would not have been defensible).

192. *1843.*

Nevertheless, the appearance of Christ is and remains a paradox. In regard to his contemporaries, the paradox lay therein that He, this definite, separate man, who looked like other men, spoke like them and observed the same customs and usages, that He was the son of God. In regard to all later ages the paradox lay elsewhere: not seeing Him with the physical eye, it was easier to imagine Him as God's son, but now comes the stumbling-block: that He spoke in conformity with the mode of thinking of a definite era. And yet, if He hadn't, it would have been a grave injustice to His contemporaries; for in that case theirs would have been the only age to have had a paradox to be shocked by. It is my opinion, at least, that His contemporaries were faced with the worst paradox, for the sentimental yearning: to have been a contemporary of Christ, which many people talk about, does not mean much, whereas actually witnessing such a paradox would be a matter of the gravest importance.

193. *1847.*

Kant's theory* on radical Evil has just one fault: he does not quite establish that the Inexplicable is a

category, that the Paradox is a category. That is
actually what it is all about. We constantly hear now:
to say that one cannot understand this or that is not
enough for science, for science desires to understand.
Here lies the fault; just the contrary should be said,
viz.: when *human* science refuses to acknowledge
that there is something it cannot understand or, still
more precisely: something it clearly understands that
it cannot understand, then all is confusion. It is
precisely the task of human apprehension to understand that there is something it cannot understand,
and also what that something is. Human apprehension generally is very busy trying to understand, to
understand more and more, but if, at the same time,
it would take pains to understand itself, it simply
has to establish the Paradox. The Paradox is not a
concession, but a category, an ontological definition
that expresses the relation between an existing, apprehending mind and eternal truth.

194.
The New Proverb   *1851.*

"I really do believe that Lying is a science," said the
Devil; he was attending lectures at Kiel university.

This amused Bishop Mynster a great deal when I
talked to him yesterday. I had it on my lips to say, but
did not utter it, for then Mynster would not have put
the proverb into circulation, which I rather wanted
him to do;—I had it on my lips to say: "That is what
I have always said: Lying is a science, Truth a paradox."

195.

The Night of the Unconditional   *1854.*

Man has an inborn terror of walking in the dark—what wonder then that he has an inborn terror of the Unconditional, of getting himself involved with the Unconditional, about which it is true that "no night and no darkness is half as black" as this darkness and this night where all relative aims (the ordinary milestones and signposts), where all mutual regards (the lanterns that generally help shed light on our way), where even the tenderest and deepest feelings of affection are extinguished, for if they aren't we are not dealing with the absolutely Unconditional.

3. FAITH AND DOUBT

196.

Primitivity   *1854.*

Every human being is born with a seed of primitivity (for primitivity means a possibility for [developing] the spirit). God who created it knows that best.

All profane, temporal, worldly intelligence has relation to destroying one's primitivity. Christianity has relation to developing one's primitivity.

Destroy your primitivity, and you will most probably get along well in the world, maybe achieve great success—but Eternity wil reject you. Follow up your primitivity, and you will be shipwrecked in temporality, but accepted by Eternity.

197.   *1854.*

By primitivity Christianity does not of course mean
the usual fanfare about the intellectual, about being
a genius and the like. No; primitivity, spirit, means
staking your life and putting the kingdom of God
first, first, first.* The more literally a person can accept this, and act accordingly, the more primitivity
he has.

198.

Wanting to be Just Like Others   *1854.*

might appear as a sort of faithfulness to these others
and, of course, is advertized and extolled as such in
the world—but it goes without saying that the direct
opposite is the case, for since ordinarily every individual, spiritually speaking, is a knave and the race
a knavish race, so the human language is first and
last a knaves' language that hypocritically turns
everything around.

No, indeed, wanting to be just like others is
cowardly, indolent dishonesty toward these others.

That is why punishment has descended upon the
race: that here these millions live who, ultimately,
are well aware mutually that all is unreliability, because one individual is always just like the next.
Therefore, observe their fear and perplexity and
suspiciousness when life gets a little tough.

On the contrary, primitivity means honesty and
fairness toward others. Anyone who has persevered
in living up to his primitivity has a reliable knowledge of existence, may be rated an able seaman on
life's ocean, has something he can vouch for. If a
blushing (oh, Socrates!) youth* turns to such a man

he will not talk a lot of moonshine, nor will he offer the youth that sham reliability: be like the others.

Maybe there is not at present in all Christendom a single kind of reliability that is rated higher than this: being like the others. It is not mentioned, of course; one speaks in the highest terms as if one possessed the highest reliability—but when catastrophe strikes everything turns out to be: like the others.

199.

The Primitive—The Traditional   *1851.*

In our day erudite doubts make their appearance more and more conspicuously and take away now one part, now another, of the Scriptures. The orthodox are in despair. Strange! The New Testament is assumed to be the word of God—but people seem to forget altogether that God must still exist, at least one would think so. The thing is: people do not believe, they ape in a historical sense *(historice).**

Suppose doubt took it into its head to present certain probable evidence that Paul's epistles were not by him, or that Paul had never existed. Then what? Well, learned orthodoxy would have to despair. The believer, quite *simplement,* would have to turn to God in prayer and say: how can one account for all this? I cannot cope with all that erudition, but I cling to the teachings of St. Paul—and Thou, oh God, wilt not let me live in erroneous delusion, no matter what the critics may prove about Paul's existence. I take what I have read of St. Paul and refer it to Thee, oh God, and Thou wilt protect me, so that what I read will not lead me into error.

I might actually be tempted to think that the Governance allows learned exegetic and critical scepticism* to get the upper hand to such a great extent, because the Governance has had enough of hypocrisy and all the monkey-business with history and the truth of the historical and wants to force men back to primitivity. For primitivity—having to be primitive, alone with God without being preceded by others whom one can ape and to whom one can refer for corroboration—is something people accept most reluctantly. And with each passing century the many millions involved in "the historical" went on increasing, and human beings became more and more spiritually dead. Then God has managed it so that the disrupting criticism gains more and more power as the centuries roll by. All deadening of spirit is bound up with this historical taking shelter and making a pretext of the innumerable millions who have lived before us.

200.

St. Stephen's Day [Boxing Day]   *1851*.
The festival of Christmas begins and ends with angels. Yesterday the angels proclaimed that a Savior had been born—today St. Stephen bears witness to it —"and they beheld his face like that of an angel." [1]
(1. *Marginal note*: "But," some will say, "angels! why, angels have never been seen; that is strictly for children." Reply: "Nonsense, rubbish, shut up—just you see to it that *you* become like *Stephanus*, that your face resembles that of an angel; in that way the rest of us will get to see an angel!")

201.   1849.

All this world-historical to-do and arguments and proofs of the truth of Christianity must be discarded; the only proof there is, is Faith. If I truly have a conviction (and that, we know, is an inner determination in the direction of spirit) my conviction to me is always stronger than reasons; actually, conviction is what *supports* the reasons, not the other way round. In that respect the exponent of the esthetic in "*Either-Or*" was right to a certain extent when he said in one of his Diapsalmata:* reasons are rather peculiar: when I have no passion I look down overbearingly on reasons, but when I have passion reasons swell to monstrous dimensions. What he is talking about, and what he calls passion, is the passionate, the innermost depth, and that is precisely what a conviction represents. A rooster can no more lay an egg—*höchstens* [at most] a wind-egg, than "reasons" can beget or give birth to a conviction, no matter how long their intercourse. Conviction has its origin elsewhere. That is what I put down somewhere in some problems, written on a sheet of paper glued on to a piece of cardboard, and what I meant to convey by the problem: On the difference between a pathetic and a dialectic transition.*

It then can never possibly occur that one keeps his conviction in the background while bringing his reasons to the fore. No, one's conviction, or the fact that it is one's conviction: my, your, conviction (the personal) is decisive. One can deal with reasons half jokingly: Well, if you insist on reasons I don't mind giving you some; do you want 3 or 5 or 7, how many do you want? Still, I cannot say anything higher than this: I have faith! I believe! That is the positive of saturation,* as when a lover says: "She is the one I love," and doesn't go on talking about it, saying that he loves her better than other men love their beloved, nor speak about his reasons for loving her.

In other words, conviction, which means personality, leads the way; reasons are relegated to a lower plane. This again is the direct opposite of all modern objectivity.

My development, or any man's, proceeds like this: Maybe he too starts out with some reasons, but they represent the lower plane. Then he makes a choice; under the weight of responsibility before God a conviction will be born in him by God's help. Now he has attained the positive. Henceforth he cannot defend his conviction or prove it by reasons; that would be a contradiction in terms, since reasons belong to the lower plane. No, the matter becomes further personal, or it becomes a question of personality, i.e. one can only defend one's conviction ethically, personally, that is through the sacrifices one is willing to make for it and by the dauntlessness with which one maintains it.

There is only one proof of the truth of Christianity: the inner proof, *argumentum spiritus sancti.**

In the Epistle of St. John (1, 5, 9) this is hinted: "If we receive the witness of men" (meaning all the historical evidence and considerations), "the witness of God is greater" i.e. the inner testimony is greater. And in verse 10: "He that believeth on the Son of God hath the witness in himself."

It is not the reasons that motivate belief in the Son of God, but the other way round, belief in the Son of God constitutes the evidence. It is the very motion of the Infinite, and it cannot be otherwise. Reasons do not motivate conviction; conviction motivates the reasons. All that went before was merely preparatory study, something preliminary, something that will disappear as soon as conviction makes its appearance and transforms everything, or turns the relationship around. Otherwise there would not be any repose in a conviction either; for then having a conviction would mean constantly repeating reasons to prove it. Repose, absolute repose in a conviction, in faith, simply means that faith itself is the evidence, "the witness," and conviction the motivation.

202. *1849.*

1. From a Christian point of view a dogmatic system is an article of luxury; in fair weather, when one can guarantee that at least an average of the population are Christians, there might be time for such a thing— but when was that ever the case? And in stormy weather the systematic is deprecated as an evil; at such times everything theological must be edifying. Indirectly the systematical contains a *falsum,* a false premise, as if all were well and all of us truly Christian, since there is time for erecting systems.

2. A dogmatic system should not be built on the basis of *understanding faith,* but on the basis of *understanding that one cannot understand faith.* The thing is that in a Christian sense "the parson" and "the professor" must say one and the same thing; only, the professor's tidings must be raised to the

second power. If there be some rebellious spirits who refuse to content themselves with "the parson," they will be served stricter fare at the professor's table. In a Christian sense all is discipline, and the higher degree is attained by undergoing stricter discipline. By running away from "the parson" one does not gain permission to slip into speculative laxity, but rather ought to come under still stricter discipline.

203.   1850.

Quarrelling with people about what Christianity is is a mistake, for with very few exceptions their tactics aim at warding off understanding or learning what Christianity is, because they suspect that it is rather easy to grasp, but also that it would interfere with their lives.

204.

The Divine—The Human   1851.

Perhaps you say: "But, after all, it was God Himself who created this world with all its beauty and joy, so He is contradicting Himself by letting Christianity come and change everything into sin and demand that we must die to the world."

In a certain sense I have nothing to reply, for such matters do not concern me. If a thing has been established as the teaching of Christianity, then I have nothing to do with such objections.

But for the rest, is it not self-contradictory to accept a part of the Bible as God's word, accept Christianity as divine teaching—and then, when confronted with something you cannot bring into accord with

your intelligence or your emotions to say that God is
contradicting Himself, whereas actually it is you who
are contradicting yourself, for either you must reject
this divine teaching entirely or put up with it just
as it is.

205.

Without "Imitation" of Christ Christianity is
Mythology, Poetry 1852.

The freethinkers of our day attack Christianity and
call it mythology, poetry.

Then its defenders, its official exponents, arrive
(the rescue-crew one might call them rather satiri-
cally, reflecting what that means in case of fire;) they
protest, curse and swear that it is horrible; to them
Christianity is anything but mythology, poetry.

Aber, aber [but, but] their expounding, viewed as
a whole, completely omits the "Imitation" (even in
their sermons they keep almost mum about that side
of Christianity), and one would say that their lives,
all their protestations notwithstanding, express practically the opposite of living up to Christ's bidding, so
to them Christianity actually *is* mythology, poetry.

There is an altogether peculiar thing about protestations in cases where, indirectly, they can be dis-
proved. If a man fumbles awkwardly with an ax, and
then assures me by all that is Sacred that he is a
cabinet-maker, I counter quite confidently: No, if a
man handles an ax like that he cannot possibly be a
cabinet-maker, notwithstanding his heated assurances
to the contrary.

VII

CHRISTENDOM

1. LUTHER AND PROTESTANTISM

206.   *1847.*

Strange! The category "For you" (subjectivity, inwardness) with which *"Either-Or"* ends (only *that* truth edifies which you feel to be the truth) is exactly like Luther's. Actually, I have never really read anything by Luther. But now I open his "Book of Homilies" and immediately in the lesson for the First Sunday in Advent I find the place where he says "For You"; that is what matters.

207.   *1848.*

What a comfort it must be to him who on hearing and reading our contemporary clergymen almost has to say to himself: "Ah, I get you; I see what I must do; all I have to do is to get a little lax, for I have already become too perfect." What a comfort it is to read Luther! Here, surely, is a man who can keep abreast of one, preach one farther away from the path instead of calling one back.

208.

Saturday (April 22, 1848).

Today I have read Luther's sermon for this date in his series. It was the gospel about the ten lepers. Indeed, that man Luther is the master of us all.

209.

When I consider Luther it often occurs to me that there is something very irregular about him: a reformer who wants to throw off a yoke: that is a precarious proposition. Precisely for that reason he was immediately taken advantage of *politically,* for he himself tended toward politics, he had a border-area there* as was also characteristic of his whole position: not to attack "the crowd," but some individual, high-ranking person.

That was why the struggle became too easy for Luther. The hardship resides in having to suffer because one must make the problem harder for others. When one is fighting to throw off burdens, of course one is right away understood by a lot of people in whose interests it is that the burden be thrown off. So here the true Christian stamp: Double-Danger, is missing.

In a certain sense Luther came to take the matter too easily. He should have made it quite clear that the freedom he fought for (and in this fight he was right) would result in making life, spiritual life, infinitely more strenuous than it was before

If he had strictly maintained *that,* he surely would not have won any adherents, and he would have faced the Double-Danger; for nobody sides with a person in order to have his life made more strenuous.

But he veered too quickly. Jubilant, politically jubilant, the contemporary age appropriated his cause, made it a party-matter;* Luther wants to overthrow the Pope—bravo! Well, thank you—that too is purely a political deal!

It is important for me to make this clear dialectically; for the rest Luther has all my respect—but a Socrates! No, no, that Luther was not by far. When I speak simply of a human being I will say: Oh, of all human beings the greatest is old Socrates, hero and martyr of intellectuality. You alone, Socrates, knew what it meant to be a reformer, understood your own self in so being; you were one.

210.
Oh, Luther   *1854.*

Luther, what a vast responsibility is yours, after all, for as I look closer I see more and more clearly that while you did overthrow the Pope, you enthroned "the Public" in his stead.

You changed the New Testament's concept of "Martyrdom," taught men to bring home victory by means of numbers.

211.
The Retreat   *1854.*

We are now about to make a withdrawal of a special kind.

The problems must be taken back to the convent from which Luther broke away—that, I believe, will probably be the truth. That is not to say, however, that the Pope will triumph now, nor will it be papal gendarmes who will have to take the problem back to the convent.

What was wrong with convents was not their ascetic aspect, celibacy, etc.; no, what was wrong was that they had been permitted to become lax about Christianity by letting the cloistered ones come to be regarded as *extra-ordinary* Christians—and purely secular rubbish as extra-ordinary Christianity.

No, asceticism and everything pertaining to it is merely the beginning, the preliminary condition for being able to bear witness to the Truth.

So Luther's veering was wrong; it was not a question of slackening the Christian demands, but of tightening them.

That is why I have always wondered whether God really was on the Lutheran side, for wherever God is present progress will be recognizable by mounting demands, by the cause becoming harder. On the other hand, the human way is always recognizable by matters being made easier; and that is called progress.

So what was wrong in the Middle Ages were not convents and asceticism; what was wrong was that *worldliness* actually achieved supremacy when monks were made to parade as extra-ordinary Christians.

No, first be an ascetic, which means gymnastics; then bear witness to the Truth, which quite simply means being a Christian—and good night, you millions, trillions and quadrillions.

Luther should have veered in that way, or he should have made it clear that by the turn he took the Christian claim was cut down even further owing to the prevailing, ever more rampant, wretchedness of the human race.

2. THE CHRISTIAN WORLD

212.

Luther—the Reformation   *1855.*

Luther is the direct opposite of "the apostle."*

"The apostle" expounds Christianity in the interests of God; he comes with authority from God and in his errand.

Luther expounds Christianity in the interests of man, actually the reaction of the human side to the Christian side representing God's interest. So that is why Luther's formula is: "I cannot do otherwise,"* which in no wise is that of an apostle.

Just look at the confusion thus wrought by making Luther an apostle.

Altogether, what Christianity has always lacked is a diagnostician* for its ailments, and then a dialectician.

213.
Protestantism   1854.

is completely untenable. It is a revolution brought about by proclaiming "the Apostle"* (Paul) at the expense of the Master (Christ).

As a corrective at a given time in given circumstances it may have had its importance.

Otherwise, if Protestantism is to be maintained at all, it would have to be done like this: We admit that this teaching represents a mitigation of Christianity which we humans have permitted ourselves, and we must ask God if he is willing to accept it.

But instead Protestantism is trumpeted about as an advance in Christianity! It is not; perhaps it is the most marked concession ever made to the Numerical, this Numerical which is Christianity's hereditary enemy, which pretends to be Christian, but wants to eliminate or reduce ideality and is defiant by dint of its great numbers.

214.

Distances 1852.

So there one of God's chosen tools went down. In hardly imaginable inner torments, in passion far, far beyond reason, with which fact his own reason in the hour of temptation and cruel doubt often enough tormented him, he held out, fighting against reason, held out in passion striving along a path where, according to reason's judgment, he could see only too clearly that in everything he stood to lose; he held out while his contemporaries regarded him as insane or as a man possessed by the devil; hated, cursed, persecuted, he finally went down, meeting a martyr's death. Thereupon a strange thing happened: as if by magic it now seems that all existence bows down to, obeys this man of torments; it turns out that he, precisely he, was right.

Now let us cover the distances.

The next generation pauses, as it were, pauses in admiration, for it is still vibrating from the powerful impression that all this happened on the other side of reason, beyond reason; with this next generation it was as when a rock is thrown into a pool: the surface does not subside immediately, but keeps on vibrating for some time, though more and more imperceptibly.

The following generation still feels admiration—though some whisperings are heard: after all, it was so inexplicable or incomprehensible; if one really thinks it over, it does not seem impossible to comprehend that Glorious Being. And this is not being said to disparage him, far from it; on the contrary, the intention is to honor him.

What does that mean? It means that people now have come so great a distance from the passionate tensions of the event that they can begin to reason calmly.

This, then, gets the upper hand and at last "the professor"* arrives on the scene. On multifarious grounds he is able to prove, corroborate and comprehend. The Glorious Deceased and his life are scientifically dissected, arranged paragraph by paragraph. Post-graduate students are examined in the question: on which grounds the Life of the Glorious One can be comprehended. And then when they have mastered it all they are appointed or "called" to a pleasant little living, with prospects of advancement, where they will expound said grounds and reasons to a congregation.

As soon as (or so, at least, it was in the old days) the Minister of State appeared in the antechamber the audience with the king was over; and as soon as "the professor" arrived it showed that the Glorious One's life was used up, a new victim would now be needed. Still, "the professor" flatters himself and the respective undergraduates, post-graduates and their future wives by asserting that he, "the professor," is Evolution's finest and richest flower.

No, Sir, that is a misunderstanding. "The professor" is the most preposterous human folly, for he represents a conceited human attempt to exhaust by reflection that which is high above reflection. The disappointing thing to the professor is that he is so far removed from being a contemporary of the Glorious One, and that the stirring emotions which the man's contemporaries felt to the point of frenzy, stirrings that vibrated in the next generation, have now subsided completely. That being so, disappointment followed, and people say that if one really would go into the matter, think and reflect, it should be possible to understand the Glorious One and His life—and that is the point where "the professor" shows up—and that means: good-bye for now—all is over until further notice.

Even in the world of individuals an analogy may be pointed out. Take a person who is deeply infatuated; during the period in which he is truly infatuated it never occurs to him that he should be able to comprehend it; rather, it seems inconceivable—oh, lovable humility—that the girl can love him. Then let him have the girl. And let the years pass—and then perhaps a time will come when he no longer trembles with passion; no, passion has quite subsided, and he has become extremely intelligent, that is to say: quite stupid. Whether he has reached that point will be recognizable by whether he thinks that for such and such a reason he will be perfectly able to understand his infatuation. This is something that often occurs in the personal world: A husband or a wife who was once in love, will ten years later be professor or lady-lecturer in his or her infatuation. As always, professors and lecturers are recognizable by their fancying themselves to be the finest bloom of the highest evolution, and so these love-professors and lady-lecturers likewise think that the phase they have now reached is the highest.

215.
The Two Paths   1854.

One thing is to suffer; another to graduate and become a professor in someone else's sufferings.

The first is "the path"; the second is "going around
it" (wherefore the preposition "around" might serve
as a motto for all lecturing and lecture-preaching),
and perhaps the "going around" may end in going
down and out.

216.
The New Testament   1854.

A young girl of "sixteen summers";*—it is her con-
firmation day. Among the many tasteful and beautiful gifts she also receives the New Testament in a
very pretty binding.

Now, that is what one may call Christianity! To
tell the truth, no one expects—and probably rightly—
that she, any more than anybody else, will read it,
or at any rate not in a primitive way. This book was
given her as a potential consolation in life; here,
should you need it, you will find consolation; of
course it is assumed that she will never read it, no
more than other young girls, but if she does, it will
not be "primitively," or she would discover that right
there in that book you find such terrors that, in comparison, other terrible things that occur in the world
are almost a joke.

Yet that is supposed to be Christianity. And of
course the foolishness with Bible Societies distributing the New Testament by the million, that too
is Christianity.

No, I would be tempted to make Christianity another proposition: Let us gather in every single copy
of the New Testament, let us cart the whole collec-
tion out to an open place, or up a mountain top, and
then, while all of us kneel down, let someone speak
to God, saying: Take it back, this book; we humans,
the way we are, should not get involved with such a
book; it only makes us unhappy. Now, I suggest that,
like those townspeople of yore, we ask Christ to take
another road. That would be talking honestly and
humanly— something else than this disgusting, hypo-
critical parson's twaddle about life being of no value
to us without the invaluable boon of Christianity.

217.

The Tame Goose—A Revivalist Reflection

1854.

Imagine what it would be like if geese could talk—
then they surely would have ordered their affairs so
that they too had their divine service, their worship
of God.

They would gather every Sunday and listen to the
gander's sermon.

The gander would dwell on the high destiny of
geese, the high goal for which the Creator had destined them—and each time His name was mentioned
the lady-geese would curtsey and the ganders would
bow their heads. Their wings would carry them away
to distant regions, blissful regions, where they truly
belonged, for on earth they were like strangers in a
foreign land.

Thus every Sunday. When the service was over the

congregation would rise and the geese waddle home.
And again next Sunday they would attend divine
service—and go home—and that would be that. They
would thrive and grow fat, become plump and tasty,
and eventually they would be eaten on St. Martin's
Eve—and that would be that.

Yes, that would be that. For while listening to
resounding sermons on Sundays, on Mondays the
geese would have a lot to tell each other, among other
things what happened to a goose who tried in earnest
to use the wings the Creator had given it, destined
for the high goal set before it; yes, what happened to
it, what horrors it had to endure. The geese, among
themselves, knew all about it. But of course it did
not behoove them to speak of it on Sundays, for, as
they said, then it would become obvious that our
worship actually is a mockery of God and of our-
selves.

There were also among the geese a few who began
to look peaked and were losing weight. Of those the
other geese said: Well, now we certainly see where
it leads: this wanting to fly in earnest. For because
they constantly have this idea of flying on their
minds they lose weight, don't thrive, don't enjoy
God's grace like ourselves, which is why we grow
plump, fat, and tasty—for God's grace makes one
plump, fat, and tasty.

And again next Sunday they would go to church,
and the older gander would preach about the high
goal for which the Creator (here the geese curtsied
and the ganders bowed their heads) had destined
them, the goal for which they had been given their
wings.

Thus with the worship of God in Christianity. Man too has wings; he has imagination. It is meant to help him really to soar—but all we do is play, we let imagination entertain us in a quiet hour, in a Sunday reverie, and for the rest we stay as we were; then on Monday we regard it as God's grace that we grow plump, fat, tasty and put on an extra layer of yellow fat, save money, acquire prestige in the world, beget many children and are successful—all this we regard as proof of God's grace. But those who really get involved with God and who therefore—it cannot be otherwise and according to the New Testament it isn't—suffer and look worried, have trouble, toil and affliction—of those we say: There, it is quite obvious that they don't enjoy the grace of God.

Then when someone reads this he will say: How fine, how very fine. And that is that—then he waddles home and strives with all his might to become plump, tasty and fat—but on Sunday the parson delivers a sermon and he listens to it—just like the geese.

3. THE CLERGY

218. *1847.*

I am well aware that in the matter of canonicals some prelates use broadcloth, others silk, velvet, bombazine, etc., but I wonder if those are the right canonicals. I wonder if the true Christian canonicals are not these: Being derided in a good cause, being scorned and spat on, the degree thereof would indicate the clergyman's order of rank. Look, surely Christ was not a suicide, so the evident conclusion is that

the guilt of the world was revealed when men crucified him. And I wonder whether the world has grown
very much better in the meantime. But to preach
about Christ decked out in finery and furbelows to a
crowd of curious gapers! Disgusting!

219.
Sermon-Lectures   1850.

They are disputing which form of sermon is the most
correct.

The thing is this: Sermons as we know them today
(i.e. oratory, rhetorics) constitute a form of communication in complete disaccord with Christianity.

Christianity can be communicated only by witnesses, i.e. by men who existentially express what
they proclaim, realize it in their lives.

At the very moments when Mynster is most brilliant and most admired he is also, from a Christian
point of view, most untruthful. Oh, frightening
thought: the same crowd that becomes dumb with
admiration would unleash its fury against a poor,
maltreated apostle—who would carry out in practice
what Mynster loftily preaches.

220.
The Test of Christendom   1850.

Order the parsons to shut up on Sundays. What
would be left? The essential, indeed! human lives,
daily life, which the parsons use for their sermons.
Then, if you look around, do you gain the impression
that what they preach is Christianity?

221. *1850.*

. . . That I am right everybody fundamentally knows —including Bishop Mynster. That it will never be admitted that I am right everybody knows too—including myself.

222.

The Clergy *1851.*

constitutes executive power. Now imagine for the sake of truly visualizing the reigning confusion, now imagine, for instance, that the police instead of acting would begin to *lecture* on stealing, etc.

223.

Fraud *1851.*

Someone assures me that it is in order to spare his fellow-men that he represents Christianity as being mild and bland; but does that mean that he is stricter with himself? No! Aha! So here again we have ambiguity: he spares himself, but wants at the same time to enjoy the benefit of being liked and loved by people because he is so gentle with them.

224.

Balderdash *1850.*

Today I was speaking with a Most Reverend. He explained enthusiastically that what he really needed was mendicant friars. Why then does the Most Reverend not become a mendicant friar himself? On that point, at least, one cannot say: "I *cannot*," as it is only a matter of will. In other words, the Most Reverend prefers staying put in a fat living. But come Sunday, he will preach a moving sermon about mendicant friars being what we really need.

And further: Suppose such a mendicant friar actually did appear among us, what would the Most Reverend do? He would immediately seize the opportunity to proclaim: "Exactly what I have always said" —and would almost imagine himself to be that friar, whereas he should realize that his guilt is the greater, the longer and the more loudmouthed he has been announcing that mendicant friars were what we needed; and then not acting accordingly.

And further: Let the mendicant friar stay among us for just one year, and the Most Reverend would be among the first to cry: "This is exaggerated—this is too much," for now it would seem that things were in earnest.

You see, this Most Reverend is safely ensconced in his large living, all the while closely watching out for a better one to become vacant which he can apply for. Perfect human balderdash! Go in for balderdash —and there you will find advancement and betterment. As for Truth: there is no advancement for Truth in this world—only retrogression.

225.

A Clergyman. My Affair.   1854.

I imagine a clergyman. In a private conversation I take it upon myself to make entirely clear to him that Christianity is non-existent. Then what? Let me tell it in the form of a vignette.

He returns to his village (he is a country parson). Back in his home he greets the family, deals with whatever business is pending—and now it is evening. After supper, talking with his wife, he remarks: "What a strange person that *Magister* Kierkegaard! I talked to him for a long time yesterday, a couple of hours I believe, and he made it absolutely clear to me that Christianity actually does not exist. A strange person indeed!"

But come Saturday, our Reverend calmly takes out the sermon on rotation (he is one of the good, honest parsons who only repeat their sermons every six years), memorizes it, and duly delivers it on Sunday morning. In the course of the year he provides his wife with yet another infant, and since it is a boy, the mother insists that he must become a student of Divinity, wherein the father concurs, already visualizing the boy as his successor in the living he now holds—

—and it is entirely clear that Christianity is nonexistent.

Oh, you asses that one must deal with! And there are millions like that—or rather, that is what human beings are like.

It does not for a moment occur to such a parson that it might mean something to him personally that Christianity is completely non-existent. As long as the State keeps on paying a salary for the twaddle parsons pour out, serve and sell under the name of Christianity, nothing worries him.

And if his wife, when he told her how clear *Magister* Kierkegaard had made it to him that Christianity did not exist, had been naive and feminine enough to say: Good Heavens, Ludvig, but how then can you be a parson—if Christianity is non-existent? all he need reply would be: Well, my good Sophia, it will probably be best for all of us if I try not to understand the matter in that sense, for I don't know whether you are able to earn a living for me and the children! And certainly nothing more is needed: in that very instant Sophia undergoes a metamorphosis: she spontaneously admits that her remark was a childish vestige from the early days when she was still a maiden, and no one approves more than she the parson's decision to let well enough alone.

226.   1848.

Mynster,* I should say, is really quite inexplicable. In one passage he will talk about the horrible confusion of the world today, and one would think Christianity was doomed. Then in the next he says that we have the great Christian festivals to remind us of what we owe to Christianity, like the Whitsun celebration now. And he will hold forth about that. Then he comes home. Otherwise he administers his office like an official of the Law.

The confusion of the times constitutes a testing of men's lives, that is what it does, and Mynster is a ship without a compass. What is Great about him is his personal virtuosity in the manner of Goethe,* which makes him conduct himself with a certain dignity. But actually his life expresses nothing.

That is why he always has been so fond of "the quiet moments in Holy places." 1) Because he distributes religion like an ingredient to be added to life, but not as an *absolute* demand; 2) because he wants to be secure within the fence of a thousand safeguards before he will open his mouth; briefly, his sermon must be a masterpiece, and his delivery of it, a triumph. 3) Because he wants to make his own life secure and keep things at a distance.

For Mynster it would be quite impossible, indeed the most impossible thing of all, to preach in the market place. Yet preaching in the churches is on the verge of becoming paganism and theatrical show-business, and Luther was substantially right in urging that there really should not be any preaching of sermons in the churches.

In the pagan era the theater stood for divine worship.

In the Christian era the churches have become regular theaters. How so? Thus: people find it pleasant, indeed quite enjoyable, once a week, like that, making contact in imagination with the Highest. Neither more nor less. And that has actually become the norm for sermons and divine worship in Denmark. Hence that artistic remoteness—even in the most bungled of sermons.

227.   *1848.*

Mynster's sermon:* the one about Joseph's foster-father.

It is deceitful, is it not, to talk in this vein: "What happens to me when I cannot ward it off, where I am led when I cannot take any other road, that is God's will." Well, thank you! that means avoiding every difficulty; the difficult part is that a man must *choose*, make his own choice. But it looks so easy and "geschwindt" [quick], this attitude which, if it were to become true in the highest sense, is met with only very, very rarely, and it sounds Luther-like: "I cannot do otherwise, God help me, Amen!" Here it is immediately evident that the man who is speaking knows what it means to make a choice.

But it boils down to this: that Mynster somehow always has been able to muddle through on half-truths; he probably never has acted outstandingly (in an eminent sense), or else he could not possibly speak as he does.

228.   1848.

Actually Bishop Mynster's merit in the way of Christianity is that through his considerable personality, his culture, his superiority, developed in the high and highest circles, he has established the fashion or, more solemnly, the accepted custom, that Christianity is something which no really deep and serious person (how flattering!), no cultivated person (how very pleasant!) can do without.

However, in an eternal and true Christian sense, this merit is somewhat equivocal. For indeed Christianity is so high-ranking on its own that it certainly needs no patronizing.

Also his earnestness has a whiff of "melange" [a brand of common, blended tobacco]—so moved, so deeply touched by the thought of those Glorious ones—yet, ah, so vulnerable and thin-skinned when it comes down to bedrock and he himself has to bear the brunt of being belittled ever so slightly.

Yet I love Bishop Mynster, and my only wish is to do everything I can to further his repute, for I have admired him and, humanly speaking, I still do; and every time I can do something that accrues to his benefit I think of my father whom, I believe, it would please.

229.   *1848.*

One would think that the whole concept of a clergy-man as lecturer, *eo ipso* would spell the abolition of Christianity. The whole thing is covered up by still deeper confusion, as one gets busy developing the idea that a clergyman must be simple, express him-self simply, not use complicated words. Pshaw! for one thing, *that* depends upon chance circumstances. No, the crux of it is that a clergyman is not to be an orator, but a man who lives according to the precepts he expounds.

But today the commonly accepted idea of a clergy-man actually helps to demoralize a congregation. There they sit, in a comfortable church, in pomp and splendor (indeed as in a theater)—then a man steps forward, an artist (for don't let us deceive our-selves: despite his protestations that he is a simple man, it actually means that he has perfected himself in the art of being simple; true simplicity means that a man practices what he preaches). So a man steps forward "clothed in soft raiment,"* in possession of all the good things of life—and that man speaks about the Highest, about being willing to sacrifice all. Oh, how smiling that appears, how utterly different from what it would be if, in earnest, he were to give up the least little thing. Oh, awful seduction, what so-phistication: to have everything—and then to lend oneself to this [Christian] spectacle as an artist.

That, you see, is why people do not recognize it. Take Paul, for instance; when he was in chains—how many among the crowd saw the lofty spirituality in him? The majority, the overwhelming majority, only saw a fanatic whom they *"höchstens"* [at most] pitied

a little. But when in the Palace Church, where all
breathes security and peace, and all is pomp and
circumstance, Bishop Mynster, an impressive figure
of a man, steps back in the pulpit, draws himself up
to his full height, and describes the scene, great as
he is *qua* artist, then we understand—indeed we almost mistake Bishop Mynster himself for—the Apostle. Oh, that is vastly demoralizing. Yet I am very
fond of Bishop Mynster, and not only because the
memory of my father attaches me to him. No, Mynster expresses the purely human in a way so masterly
that I never have seen the like. On the other hand,
I should think that he is so alien to what is essential
in Christianity that, if he should make a definition
thereof he probably would have to say: It is the
Demoniacal.

230.   1849.

In the splendid Palace Church a stately court chap-
lain, the declared favorite of the cultivated public,
shows himself to a select circle of distinguished, cultivated persons and preaches a moving sermon on
this word by the Apostle: "God chose the lowly and
despised." And nobody laughs.

231.

Martensen's Dogmatics   1849.

While all around us existence is disintegrating, while
anyone with eyes to see must discover that it is a
complete sham—all these millions of Christians, that,
on the contrary, Christianity is on the way out—Martensen is busy drawing up a system of dogmatics.
Now, what does it mean, his being busy with such

things? It means, as far as the Christian faith is concerned, since everything in this country is in apple-
pie order—here we are all Christians, no danger
threatens, we have an opportunity to indulge in
scientific studies; so, now that everything else is in
order, the important thing is to find out under which
category in the dogmatic system the doctrine on
angels should be classified, and matters like that.

232.   *1849.*

Christianity tends in everything toward realization,
to being made a practical reality, the only medium to
which it is truly related. It will not be possessed in
any other way than in realization, will not be communicated save for edification or awakening. It must
constantly be assumed that there are some who have
not got it, or are lagging behind: then work must be
undertaken for their sakes. But Christianity should
never be communicated in the medium of tranquillity
(unless the person who does it would dare to assert
that now all and everyone are Christians). That is
why being busy with art, poetry, philosophy, science
and lecturing constitutes a sin in the Christian sense
—for how dare I indulge myself* pottering about
with such things in peace and quiet?

Martensen, who has taken it upon himself to find
approximate terms and definitions, now also talks
about the idea that Christianity must be carried out
in real life—here he becomes assertive—must become
a true, real life, yes, a truly true real life within us;
our relation to Christianity must not be by way of
our imagination. Fine. But what about Martensen's
own life, what does that express? It expresses that

he wants to succeed in the world, win honors and prestige, high office, etc.—is *that* realizing Christianity?

As a philosopher Martensen is assertive, there is nothing of the dialectician about him, and as a Christian he is also merely assertive. Full of rhetorical categories—very apt to captivate people.

As for me, I am a little more of a poet, insofar as I have had the courage to dare to expose myself to ridicule and have withstood it. But I am favored by having independent means. I don't think I am able to do more. I am stepping back, but with God's help I shall retain an enthusiastic picture of those who were able to do more.

233.   *1851.*

Back from a trip abroad, returned at the opportune moment with Hegel's philosophy, he made a big sensation, had extraordinary success, won over the entire undergraduate-body to his view and to "the system," which even threatened, alas, to make my revered Bishop Mynster superfluous. Then he had a splendid official career, held high office, secured his material existence in every way, also by means of what, according to our conditions, were powerful connections; later, moreover, as a high-ranking prelate he made contact with the entire cultivated world. I was nothing and rose to nothing, but abandoned myself to the—also financially speaking—expensive pleasure of being a writer in Denmark; then I became even less than nothing: the butt of laughter and ridicule; this in turn was used against me by

higher-ranking envy, for these people refused to
understand, which I suppose they couldn't know
either, that my course of action was dictated by
something religious; still they would not understand
that it nevertheless was a respectable course I took
in regard to our demoralized, literary conditions. I
disagreed with Prof. Martensen when he expounded
his "system," and he, I surmise, disagreed with me,
since "the public opinion" which he and "the higher
circles" commanded always decreed that what I did
and offered was something antiquated. For my part
I expressed my disagreement through my pseudonyms,* but in such an attenuated, recondite form
that the scene might as well have been laid in Germany; at that time the "Privat-Dozent" [lecturer or
assistant professor] was a stock character there, while
in Denmark we had no such bird. Martensen's name
was never mentioned, all was kept within a fictional
frame, which satisfied me as a writer and made me
happy, because I knew what a great friend of peace
he is, the Old One among us, Sealand's Most Reverend Bishop. But Martensen could not keep quiet;
in the preface to his Dogmatics he could not resist
giving me a small rap.* But why a small rap? Either
hit me hard, or keep quiet!

(Still and all, he may have to pay a high price for
that rap.)

234.

Vignette 1849.

A theologian, but so far without a living. For a number of years he has worked very hard and has attained
a measure of fame which definitely will ensure that

everyone will rush to hear him preach in church, particularly all the higher-ups.

He announces that he is going to preach and selects the finest, most splendid church in the capital.

Everyone is in church, including the King and Queen.

He mounts the pulpit, offers up a prayer; reads his text, which is about Christ chasing the money-lenders from the temple.

Immediately after that he says:

Now let the word be spoken, the word I have to say in the world, for which I have prepared myself all my life, now let the word be spoken: to preach Christianity in surroundings like these is not Christianity, be it ever so Christian, it is not Christianity; Christianity can be preached only by its being realized in the lives we live. And hereby I change this house into real life. I am now in your power, I, just one man, but now I will speak—and it will be reality. I will speak about this thing that Christianity can be preached only by living it.

Attack on the whole prettified church and the prettified congregation. Christ was not a prettified man, who in a prettified church to a prettified congregation delivered a sermon on Truth that is being made to suffer—he was *spat* upon, and it was real.

Uproar throughout the church; the congregation cry: Down with him, throw him out! But the preacher rises and speaks out in a voice of thunder that drowns out all the clamor: You see, now it is right; now I am preaching Christianity. Had they suspected my intention, I would have been prevented from mounting the pulpit here, or else you would all have stayed home. But now I stand here, now I am speaking and I make you responsible before God; you must hear me out, for it is the Truth that I am speaking.

Now, there you have an awakening!

VIII

THE CATASTROPHE

235.

Bishop Mynster March 1, 1854.

Now he is dead.*

If one could have influenced him enough at the end of his life for him to have made the admission to Christianity that what he represented was not really Christianity, but an attenuated form of it: that would have been very desirable, for he carried a whole contemporary age on his shoulders.

Therefore the possibility of such an admission had to be kept open till the last, indeed to the very last, in case he should make it on his death-bed. Therefore he must never be attacked; therefore I had to put up with everything (even when he did the desperate thing in connection with Goldschmidt),* for who could know whether it might not produce the re-action of moving him to proffer that admission.

Now that he is dead without having made the admission, everything is changed. Now all he left behind is that he preached Christianity to a standstill in an illusion.

Also in regard to my melancholy devotion to my late father's bishop, things have changed; for indeed it would be asking too much if, after his death, I should not be allowed to speak about him with less reserve, though I am entirely aware that there probably always will remain a residue of something seductive in my old devotion and esthetic admiration [of him].

Originally my wish had been to transform everything of mine into a triumph for Mynster. As I later realized, it continued to be my wish; yet I had to demand this small admission from him, something I did not desire for my own sake and which, therefore, as I thought, might well be managed so as to appear a triumph for Bishop Mynster.

From the time when a hidden misunderstanding came between us, it was my wish that I might at least succeed in avoiding attacking him while he was still among the living, but I reflected that I myself could die first.

And yet it was a close, a very close call: I believed I would have to attack him. Only one sermon of his did I miss: his last. It was not illness that prevented me, on the contrary, that Sunday I attended church under Kolthorf.* Hearing him was a signal that told me: "Now is the time to act; you must break the tradition from your father's time"—and on that very Sunday M. preached his last sermon. God be praised; it almost looks like an act of Providence.

If Bishop M. had been able to give in (which nobody need have known about) and it had been considered a triumph for him, then my outer circumstances could also have become more carefree; for Bishop M., who in his own mind did, I believe, give me some credit on the score of mind and spirit, cal-

culated in his worldly cleverness, that in the end I
would probably have to give in to him in some way
or other because, financially, I could not outlast him.
A casual remark that he quite often repeated in
conversation—without aiming it directly at me—was
rather characteristic: What counts is not who is
strongest, but who can last longest.

236.
Causing a Catastrophic Effect   1855.
How frightened people would become of me, if they
learned about it, how alien the idea would seem to
them: nevertheless, it is true that what has lately occupied my mind is whether God's will with me might
not be that I stake my all to bring about a catastrophe, so that I might be arrested, sentenced, nay, if
possible, executed. And in my soul I worry whether,
if I fail to do it, I shall not regret it eternally, against
which I can only put up the thought in which my
trust in God always rests: that He will preserve me
from failing to do something which I should eternally
regret not having done.

If I were to cause a catastrophic effect I imagined
it like this: After keeping completely silent for a
time I would quite unexpectedly make "the Outcry"
that the official worship of God is blasphemy, tantamount to sharing in a crime.

But before I had clarified this properly in my own
mind, something else occurred, as I issued the article
against Martensen on Mynster. That, already, served
to weaken the possible effect of a catastrophic "Outcry." *

Furthermore, going over the article ("The Out-cry") I see that I always intended to follow it up with some explanatory pamphlets which, again, would weaken my catastrophic effect.

Then, in regard to myself, I could not help wondering whether—if it could be managed—I actually would be any good at going to jail, and eventually being executed; whether this whole method of fighting would not have so disturbing an effect upon me that I would not be able to carry it through.

However, that I would have to leave to God.

But in regard to causing a catastrophic effect, quite a different scruple crops up. It cannot really be achieved in the way I had imagined. The present state of affairs is so demoralized that one might spit right in its eye, and it would still prefer sneaking off, taking good care not to start legal action, etc. That has been my experience; actually I have already operated in the direction of the catastrophic, for if anyone (in the present state of affairs) had the slightest intention of bringing a law-suit, my last article against Martensen certainly would have provided a test.

However, if it is true that the present state of affairs is so sunk in wretchedness and so demoralized that it is fully conscious of it all being a lie, that at no price would it dare to resort to legal procedures, such as sueing, arresting, executing, then it is definitely dangerous to have aimed my sights at it; even though the counterpart were a spot of snot, one could easily frustrate one's entire future operations. Then too, it would almost be a pity for the congrega-

tion; after all, it is terrible to reflect that on Sundays
(as happens now, by the way) everything would go
on as usual, even *after* I had told them with the
greatest emphasis that it amounted to mockery of
God. Martensen's habitual silence really constitutes
a horrible prostitution, nay, blasphemy, and the congregation would actually have to say (to Martensen)
as Countess Orsini* said to Marinelli: "Have mercy,
please, and tell a small lie; after all, that is better
than this kind of silence."

So if one wanted to act by provoking a catastrophe,
the matter would have to be tackled quite differently
from what I have had in mind hitherto.

The procedure would then be something like this:

One would begin by demonstrating that the matter
was so serious that all scholastic bickerings amounted
to childishness. So one would demand—demand in
the name of Christianity—that those representing the
status quo use all available means to defend it.

Consequently, one would have to insist on being
sued, ask to be arrested, demand that the powers-
that-be proceed with the greatest possible severity,
even to the point where it would become a matter
of life and death.

The charges against the present state of affairs
would be summed up thus: Everything is a lie, worship of God is blasphemy, to take part in it, a crime;
but the charges would be aggravated by proof that
"the present state of affairs" is aware that it is a lie,
and that is why it must avoid taking legal action
against me.

Though even so, I do not really believe it would

be possible to induce them to arrest me, let alone execute me.

Oh, but how terrible to realize to what depths the present state of affairs has sunk, to what depths of wretchedness and Philistine snobbery, mediocrity and mendacity.

Yet precisely for those reasons, what a shining light it would be for future generations: an incomparable epigram on the present state of affairs: if Bishop Mynster were buried as a witness to Truth, one of the true witnesses to the Truth.

237.
To die to the World.   July 2, (1855).

Even a courageous person does not feel easy in his mind when the dentist takes out his instruments and is about to pull out a tooth. And even the most courageous person has a strange feeling around his heart when the surgeon takes out his instruments and is about to amputate that person's arm or leg.

Yet in every man there is something that is more firmly rooted than even the most firmly embedded molar, and something to which he cleaves more strongly than to an arm or a leg of his own body: that is, his urge to live.

Therefore all experience cries out to man: Whatever you do, see to it that you don't lose your vital urge; whatever else you lose in life, if only you keep that, there will always be a chance of winning back everything.

God looks at it differently. Above all, He says, I must deprive man of his love of life, if there is to be any possibility of his becoming a Christian in earnest, of his dying to the world, hating himself and loving me.

Therefore it is terrible when God takes out his instruments for the operation which no human power has the ability to perform: to wrench from a man his vital urge, to kill him off, that he may live like one already dead.

Yet it cannot be otherwise, or else a human being cannot love God. He must live in such a state of anguish that if he were a pagan he would not hesitate for a moment to commit suicide. In that state then he must—live! Only in that state can he love God. I do not say that everyone who is in that state must needs love God, by no means; I only say that this state is a necessary condition for being able to love God.

And this religion has become a national religion: 1000 sworn Falstaffs or Animal-Doctors [veterinarians] with their families, etc. obtain their living from it.

238.
To be a Christian   July 2, *(1855)*.

Of all torments, being a Christian is the most terrible; it is—and that is how it should be—to know hell in this life.

What is a human being most terrified of? Most likely of dying, and most of all of the death-agony, therefore wishing it to be as brief as possible.

But to be a Christian means to be in a state of dying— (you must die off, hate yourself)—and yet, after that, you have to live on, maybe for 40 years, in that state! (We shudder to read about the sufferings a beast undergoes when it is used for vivisection; yet this gives only a glimmering of the pain involved in being a Christian: to be kept alive in a state of death.)

That is not all, however; there is a further aggravation. Those who surround a dying man's couch do not generally guffaw loudly at him because he groans in his last agony. Nor do they usually hate, curse, or loathe him because of that. But this torment forms an integral part of being a Christian; it comes along whenever true Christianity is to be expressed in this world.

Add to this the sore doubts* that assail a Christian in which the possibility of offense is present, seeking at every instant to avail itself of an opportunity for scandal:* viz. that this is supposed to be God's love; this is supposed to be the God of Love about whom, since childhood, you have been told everything but this!

And yet He is love, infinite love, but He can only love you if you are dying, and yet it is mercy, infinite mercy having eternal torment changed into temporal torment.

But woe unto them, the hosts of sworn liars, woe unto them, that they have taken the keys to Heaven, and not only refuse to enter themselves, but also prevent others from entering.

239.

Life here below is meant to be Christian

Sept. 25, 1855.

The purpose of life here below is to carry us to the highest degree of *taedium vitae.*

He who then, brought to this point, can hold fast, or he whom God helps to be able to hold fast the thought that it is God, who by His love has brought him to this point: he, in a Christian sense, has passed the test of life, has become ripe for Eternity.

I came into being through a crime against God's will. The offense which, in one sense, is not mine, though it makes me a criminal in the sight of God, was to give life. The penalty corresponds to the offense: being deprived of all lust for life, being brought to the highest degree of *taedium vitae*. Man wanted to imitate the handiwork of God, if not by creating man, at least by passing on life. "You will be made to pay for it, for the purpose of this life is —by my mercy, for only to those who are saved do I show that mercy—to carry you to the highest degree of *taedium vitae*."

Most human beings* are now so bereft of spirituality, so abandoned by Grace, that the punishment is not applied to them at all. Lost in this life they cling to this life; from being nothing they become nothing; their lives are wasted.

Those who retain some spirituality and are not completely overlooked by Grace, are brought to the point where they experience the highest degree of *taedium vitae*. But they cannot reconcile themselves to it and rebel against God, etc.

Only those who, brought to this point of *taedium vitae*, are able by the Grace of God to hold fast to the thought that God acts from love, so that, in their soul, not even in its innermost recesses, there is left no hidden doubt that God is indeed love: only those are ripe for Eternity.

Those are the very souls God will receive in Eternity. For what does God want? He wants souls able to praise, worship, extol and thank him—the business of angels. For the kind of beings—which are *legio* in "Christianity"—who for 10 rixdollars will bawl and blow the trumpet in honor and praise of God, that kind finds no favor with Him. Indeed no. But the angels please Him. And what pleases Him even more than the angels extolling Him, is a man, who as his time is running out, when God, as it were, transforms Himself into absolute cruelty and with the most cruelly planned cruelty does everything to rob him of any inclination to live, yet persists in believing that God is love, that God is doing it all to him from love. Such a man will become an angel. And in Heaven it will be easy for him to extol God; but, as we know, the period of apprenticeship, of schooling, is always the hardest time. Like a man who took it into his head to travel across the world to hear a singer with a perfect tone, so God sits in Heaven and listens. And every time He hears a human being whom He had brought to the extremest point of *taedium vitae*, extol Him, God says to Himself: Ah, here is the tone! He says: "Here it is," as though He were making a discovery; and yet He was prepared for it, for He Himself was present and close to this human being and helped him, insofar as God can assist in what can only be accomplished in freedom;* only free will can accomplish it; but there is amazement at being able to express oneself by thanking God for it, as if it were God who had achieved it, and in his joy at being able to do it this man is so happy that he will hear Nothing, Nothing about it being his own doing, but refers everything to God in gratitude, praying God that it may stay that way: that it is God Who does it, for this man does not believe in himself, but believes in God.

———————

NOTES

The dates of the entries are Kierkegaard's own, including the rather casual way he had of placing them, sometimes at the top, sometimes at the bottom.
the entry.

As to entries which Kierkegaard left undated, the editor has provided their respective years, printed *in italics* above
The key to references in the Notes citing *Danish* titles is as follows:

> S. V. I, 17 = *Samlede Værker* [Collected Works]
> First edition, p. 17
> VII¹ A 310 = Kierkegaards Papirer [Kierkegaard's
> Papers]
> Vol. 7, Section I, Group A. No. 310.

[These citations will then be useful primarily to students who know, or are learning, Danish.] Ordinarily, foreign words are explained only if they present some special difficulty; otherwise the reader must consult dictionaries and encyclopedias.

3. This vignette appears in a more elaborate form in *Either-Or*. (S. V. I, 26.)

5. *The Bridge of Sighs*: refers to *il ponte dei sospiri* in Venice, the closed bridge leading from the Doges' Palace to the dreaded lead dungeons, *i piombi*, which condemned men had to cross.

10. *Cf. Either-Or* (S. V. I, 4) where K. has treated the

same subject differently and more succinctly for greater stylistic effect.

"Life and Spirit" refers to a line: "To us His word is life and spirit" from the hymn by N. F. S. Grundtvig: "The Lord hath visited His people" (*Sangværk* [hymnal] I, 1837, No. 23).

12-13. From the viewpoint of the Romantic Age K. satirized the Philistine bourgeois and their moral evaluations that completely prevented them from understanding the great or the gifted, whether deviating from the norm or not. At the time K. was interested in such talented, though abnormal, figures as "the master thief," "Don Juan" and "the wandering Jew" [Ahasverus].

Gnostic Sect: K. refers to the secret sect of the Carpocratians, whose aim it was to rise above all religions, including ordinary morality, and even went so far as to believe man should commit every possible sin in order to know what it involved. Gnosticism (from Greek *gnosis*=knowledge) was a philosophical religion of salvation that originated in the first century B.C. *"Wer niemals . . ."*: Popular German song for social occasions contained in *"Visebog indeholdende udvalgte danske Selskabssange med Tillæg af nogle svenske og tyske"* [Selections of Danish songs for social occasions with some additional Swedish and German songs], collected, printed and published by Andreas Seidelin, 1814.

14. *Freedom of Speech*: These were the years when the Liberal Opposition was fighting to obtain greater freedom of the press, while the king was planning to introduce censorship. "The Society for the Proper Use of Freedom of the Press" was founded in 1835.

16. *Old Ballad*: Refers to a well-known folk song entitled "It was on a Saturday night and I was waiting for thee . . ." The second and third stanzas [in unrhymed translation] go something like this:

I lay down on my bed
and wept so bitterly;
whenever the door was opened
I thought it would be thee.

I rose on Sunday morning
and wept so bitterly,
I wanted now to go to church
to see thy dear, dear face.

The edition K. used was "Danske Folkeviser og Melo-
dier" [Danish folk ballads and melodies] collected by Fr.
Sneedorff-Birch. First pentad, containing five Jutland
ballads with melodies. 1837.

18. *Incarnation*: (Latin caro, carnis = flesh, body)
means assuming bodily form, especially about Christ's
incarnation. "*I have no pleasure in [these days]*": (Eccle-
siastes 12, 1): "Remember now thy Creator in the days of
thy youth while the evil days come not, nor the years
draw nigh when thou shalt say, I have no pleasure in
them."

20. Further developed in *Either-Or* (S. V. I, 9).

24. This piece was included in a slightly modified form
in "*Concluding Unscientific Postscript*," 1846 (S. V. VII,
391 f.) "*Den Frisindede*" [The Liberal] described as a
"Weekly of miscellaneous contents," 1835-46.

Freischütz: German weekly published in Hamburg,
1839 ff.

25. Included in *Postscript* (S. V. VII, 386) in the section on "the essential expression of existential pathos:
suffering denoting the life of a poet suffering in body
and mind as his life is ebbing out in the agony of death."
But it also expresses a torment which is not the real
visitation, for (as developed in the sequence): the sufferer still conceives his visitation or illness as something

incidental, which he would like to, and maybe can, get rid of, whereas to the soul, to the religious mind, the suffering is real because it will endure for ever.

27. *Epigram*: See Note to No. 72.

28. The first rotary printing-press was constructed for *The* [London] *Times* in 1846. Denmark's first railway was inaugurated in 1847, and the first pledges of free constitutions were given in the revolutionary year of 1848, also in Denmark.

30. *"an old hymn"*: Kierkegaard always quoted from memory, and not very exactly. The hymn is believed to be by Niels Pedersen (d. 1634) and is printed in P. Hjort: "Old and New Hymns," Second edition, 1840, p. 301. The first verse [in unrhymed translation] goes something like this:

> A bedchamber is now my grave,
> There I shall rest my body.
> On Judgment Day I'll rise again,
> I dare not doubt it.
> Go in, my soul,
> And rest full well,
> Let Evil pass you by—
> Close tight the door—
> When God so wills,
> You rise to light again.

31. *Prostitute oneself*: debase oneself.

32. *Dean Swift*, Jonathan: 18th century British [Irish] cleric and satirist, author of *Gulliver's Travels*, died insane. He bequeathed his fortune to the building of an insane asylum. K.'s rather misconstrued account was derived from the German writer J. G. Hamann. The note is repeated in *Stages on Life's Way* (S. V. VI, 189, ff.) where it is also cited as a journal entry, but developed

in greater detail. Thus the introductory paragraph about Swift, which in the papers appear rather unmotivated, is repeated, thereby rounding off the whole entry more artistically.

Quiet despair: Despair was a concept into which K. probed deeply and dealt with descriptively in *The Sickness unto Death* (1849). In fact, the sickness is despair which he sees as an ailment in man's eternal being, in the spirit, the ego, caused by man wanting to be something different from what he is destined to be by virtue of his eternal being. As a concept "Quiet despair" comes closest to the kind of despair which in the above-mentioned work is termed "the despair that knows it is despair," in other words is conscious of having "a self that does something eternal, but which now despairingly either desires not to be itself or despairingly desires to be itself,"—and within that group in turn represents "despairingly not to wish to be itself, the despair of weakness" (S. V. XI, 161 ff). It expresses itself in reserve, in "closing oneself in" [self-isolation is another term], the opposite of spontaneity. (*Cf.* Nos. 15 and 41.)

34. Back from a summer vacation in Gilleleje [on the sea of Kattegat in North Sealand] K. had found his father in a state of deep contrition of soul and of momentary mental derangement, during which he revealed certain secrets about his life that made a deep impression on his son who already (cf. No. 33) suspected that there were hidden abysses in the old man's mind. What these were which, unbeknownst to himself, he revealed in his son's presence, we do not know with certainty. Possibly they had to do with the condition mentioned in No. 43, but might also refer to certain irregularities of a sexual nature: for instance, that the father had intercourse with a maid-servant a few months after the death of his first wife and married her when it became apparent that she was pregnant. However, he placed her at a great dis-

advantage in his will and demanded separation as to property in a special marriage pact. Their first child was born some four months after the wedding in 1797.

35. Other children followed in 1799, 1801, 1805, 1807, 1809, and, as a little late-comer, Søren Kierkegaard was born in 1813, the last child in the family. The father was then 57 years old, and in a journal entry from S. K.'s last year before he died, the anger erupts which had been smoldering in him all through his life, as he assumed that his own physical defect might have been caused by his having been begotten by an old man who neither had enough vital force left to produce healthy offspring, nor enough self-control to master his sexual urge. These circumstances gave rise to a conviction in both father and son that, as a penalty, the family would become extinct and the children would die young, while the aged father would survive them all. These notions were corroborated by a number of deaths that followed in close succession, as three children died in 1832, 1833 and 1835, and the mother in 1834.

K's shaken trust in his father caused him to neglect his university studies, and he flung himself into a life of dissipation marked more by desperation than by *joie de vivre*.

37. *E. Boesen*: (Emil) was a boyhood friend of S. K. and was at his bedside when he died. About their friendship and correspondence, *cf*. Carl Koch. "Søren Kierkegaard and Emil Boesen. Letters and Introduction with a Supplement," 1901.

"a deeply faithful friend"—an old-time expression for close affection.

38. *The big earthquake*: i.e. that his father died before S. K. and that the notions they had shared about the family dying out and the old man surviving them all proved to be wrong. This impelled K. to reconsider his

life task in a new light. The true meaning of the entry
may quite easily be misconstrued, as K. chiefly refers to
a period preceding his father's death and not to "the
earthquake" proper. "Then I suspected . . ." therefore
means: "at the time," viz. before his father's death. However, *cf.* also No. 41, where it is expressly mentioned that
the quake means his father's death. (*Cf.* Carl Weltzer:
Peter and Søren Kierkegaard, I, 136 ff. and Sejer Kühle:
Søren Kierkegaard—Childhood and Youth, 171 ff.)

39. "*that I might prosper and live long in the land*,"
cf. Ephesians 6, 3 ("that it may be well with thee and
thou mayest live long on the earth," a variant on the
Second Book of Moses, Exodus) 20,12 ("Honor thy
father and thy mother that their days may be long upon
the land which the Lord thy God giveth thee.")

"*the historical continuity of domestic family life.*" As
the sins of the fathers would fall upon the children
through the third and fourth generations, the sin that
crushed the father and fell upon his son as melancholy
and despair would make it impossible for him to establish a normal family life, and thus the curse would be
perpetuated.

40. *Sibbern*, Fr. Chr.: philosopher; from 1813 professor
at the university of Copenhagen. He founded a life-or-
personality philosophy in sharp contrast to Hegel's system, which influenced the poet Poul Møller as well as
S. K. Sibbern's outlook on life was very finely expressed
in *The Posthumous Letters of Gabrieli* (1826), the style
of which influenced S. K. in his esthetic writings and in
the edifying discourses. Though S. K. disliked Sibbern's
religious humanism, poised optimism, and interest in
social problems, he had to respect his university teacher's
fairmindedness and his demand for individual penetra-
tion and depth in the matter of achieving a personal
religious and philosophical conviction.

Peter Christian Kierkegaard was S. K.'s older brother, b. 1805. He became bishop at Aalborg, Jutland, was an adherent of N. F. S. Grundtvig [great Danish poet and revivalist] and on several occasions marked his disapproval of his brother's religious views. In turn S. K. cavilled at Peter in his diaries; yet in many ways they resembled each other. Like Søren, Peter bore the imprint of the crushing atmosphere in their father's house; like Søren, he was a powerful dialectician, "der Disputierteufel aus dem Norden" [the Debating-Devil from the North] as his German fellow-students used to call him while he was studying at the universities of Berlin and Goettingen. At the same time he was of a deeply emotional religious disposition. (*Cf.* Carl Weltzer: Peter and Søren Kierkegaard, 1936.)

41. *Secret: Cf.* the diarist's note quoted on the fly-leaf of the present volume.

42. S. K. passed his final theological examination in July 1840, and immediately thereupon, in fulfillment of a pledge to his father, made a trip to the latter's native locality, Saedding in Jutland, south of Ringkøbing fiord, not far from Nymindegab. "His last wish for me" refers to the final exam which S. K.'s father wanted him to pass.

43. *"Whither shall I flee from Thy presence?" Cf.* David's Psalms: 139, 7-9.

44. When, in 1865, the editor of the first edition of S. K.'s posthumous papers showed this entry to Peter, the latter burst into tears and said: "That is my father's story—and ours too." (H. P. Barfod: "In memory of Bishop Peter Chr. Kierkegaard," 1888, p. 13.)

47. *"such an intention,"* i.e. S. K.'s desire to improve, of which the immediately preceding entries give many evidences. He had again been cultivating his lighter social side and was shining by his brilliant wit. But he

felt the emptiness of it all and realized that he was be-traying his own self—"reigning in the world, though dethroned in my inner domain." He went to call on his friend Peter Rørdam, who lived with his mother and sisters in Frederiksberg [a suburb very close to Copenhagen], in order to meet the youngest sister Bolette, for whom he seems to have entertained certain feelings which she reciprocated. But,—"for what is a man profited if he shall gain the whole world, etc." St. Matthew 16,26 . . . *when Thou overtook me, oh Lord*: God forestalled him, preventing his going to Bolette and thus giving in to his erotic urge. In other words, he turned around and headed back home.

48. Still, the following day he went to see her after all; only this time he met *Regine Olsen*, 14, daughter of Titular State Councilor Olsen. They immediately felt attracted to each other, but his feelings were mingled with fear, perhaps because he was thinking of the curse on his kin and of his own presumed early demise which would make it impossible for him to tie down a woman. Or maybe his fear was owing to conditions about which his diary keeps silent (*cf.* the diarist's note cited on the fly-leaf of the present volume).

50. *regina* (Latin): queen.
polarically: by virtue of contrasting conditions.
eccentric premises: (the opposite of concentric—having the same center) various, casual presuppositions.
or do you order me to be on my way? This means: is there a divine command which S. K. must obey, urging him on to other goals and making it impossible for him to marry? S. K. was beginning to ponder the possibility that he might be chosen for some special task or mission and therefore would be "an exception," "the chosen one," and consequently not able "to realize the univer-sal" [human lot] by marrying.

51. Fragments of a rather long account of S. K.'s relationship with Regine which he wrote in his diary in 1849 under the title: *My Relation to "Her."*

called at her house: at State Councilor Olsen's.

by lending them books . . . : like the seducer in *Either-Or* (S. V. I, 333) .

Schlegel, Fritz S., Regine's teacher whom she later married.

doing penance: a penitent (Lat. poena=penalty, a fine) repentant.

vita ante acta: former way of life.

"A psychological Experiment": "Guilty"–"Not-Guilty."

An account of suffering. Psychological Experiment by Frater Taciturnus in *Stages on Life's Way*, May 8, Morning. (S. V. VI, 308-9) which contains the letter in question ("the note") whereby S. K. formally broke off the engagement.

not unsocratically: showing a sense of simple logic.

the young man in Constantin Constantius: *The Repetition*. "An essay in experimental psychology by Constantin Constantius." (1843. S. V. III, 224 f.)

Melange: a blend, i.e. of a more earnest nature than preached by the clergy. Actually a term for a brand of blended tobacco. (*Cf.* S. V. VII, 381.)

push her boat from shore: the literal translation of Danish "støde fra" is: shove off, (repel her) making S. K. appear a cad and a cynical seducer.

The book's date and dedication: May 5, 1843, which marked S. K.'s thirtieth anniversary.

55. τελος, (Greek) =goal, purpose, aim. While S. K. at this time vaguely discerned a higher purpose for his life compared to which all other goals became unessential and, if need be, would be sacrificed (e.g. his engagement) his groping attempts to explain himself to Regine to her must have appeared like hair-splitting sophisms=Jesuitism.

56. *in a cabin*: Shortly after the final break with Regine S. K. went to Berlin and stayed for some six months to regain his balance. He left by steamer for Kiel on Oct. 25, and the four entries were written at sea.

then I went out and wept bitterly: cf. Luke, 22, 62; "And he [Peter] went out and wept bitterly."

57. *Poul Møller is dead*: He died March 13, 1838. During his college days S. K. had attended Poul Møller's lectures on philosophy (e.g. on Socrates and Aristotle) wherein the latter expressed his enjoyment of the primitive, spontaneous Greek mode of thinking and speaking in contrast to Hegel's "clever," complicated, system-structures. P. M. himself sought a form wherein, like the Greeks, he could speak "intimately" to his readers. In his last year he found such a form and used it in his dissertation entitled "Thoughts on possible evidence of man's immortality." In this he began settling accounts with the Hegelian "system," continuing the vital [existential] philosophy founded by Sibbern, which S. K. carried further forward, and which today is found as an outstanding trend of our contemporary age under the name of Existentialism.

58. *Nielsen*, N. P.: A famous actor and declaimer known from I. L. Heiberg's caricature in Act 4 of *A Soul after Death*.

59. *thoroughly polemicized*: Polemically turned in every direction. The truth of this assertion was indirectly admitted by S. K. himself. (*Cf.* No. 61.)

60. *Molbech*, Christian, Danish man of letters; from 1829 professor of literature; for a time also co-director of the Royal Theater in Copenhagen. A most productive, though not very profound writer, whose greatest merit resided in his numerous compilations, e.g. *Danish Glossary* (1833) to which S. K. referred.

Dialectician: (Greek: *dialegomai*—I converse with someone.) A person who takes a dialectic view of existence or applies a dialectic method. The idea harks back to Socrates who made his definitions of concepts in the guise of dialogues. In S. K. dialectics must be understood as his recognition that existence may be regarded from different angles, e.g. from an esthetic, an ethical or religious viewpoint either leading to a relativistic view or compelling a choice. Sometimes "dialectic" is used in the sense of logic, as in the term "architectonic-dialectical," i.e. something that appears to the eye as harmoniously proportioned, or sounds to the ear as fine rhythm.

61. *Foreword* to *Two Edifying Discourses* (1843) (S. V. III, ii) which is a dedication to "the separate individual whom with joy and gratitude I call *my reader.*"

62. *Pseudonyms*: Most of S. K.'s works were published pseudonymously, but he often stressed that opinions expressed by his pseudonyms must not be ascribed to him. (S. V. VII, 545: "In the pseudonymous books there is not one word of my own." Nevertheless there is an intimate connection between the pseudonyms and S. K.'s own self; they represent splinters of his personality, possibilities which his melancholy had conjured up in his mind over the years and which he sublimated through creative writing. However, it was only gradually that he realized this, and it is therefore literally correct when he later declared that his writing was his religious education (*Viewpoints on my activity as an author*). As long as all these fictional possibilities remained unreleased within him he was not able "to say thou to himself," could not apprehend God spontaneously, nor accept his own inner self, since the self has its origin in God. As to the various pseudonyms and what they represent in S. K.'s writings, see Hohlenberg: *The Path of the Lonely One*, p. 12-44.

63. *Mynster*: *cf.* note on No. 226.
    constitutes my innermost existence: (*Cf.* note on fly-

leaf) That which "essentially has filled my life," but which is not mentioned anywhere in S. K.'s papers and, therefore, could not be mentioned to Mynster either.

64. *that which we read . . .* in the New Testament: "that men surrender their lives and are entirely dependent upon God"—instead of looking for office. S. K. who was on the point of exhausting his private means through devoting himself to writing, and hence was thinking of stopping, and seek a parson's living instead (he could not be both writer and parson; *cf.* No. 63) here defends his right to continue as a writer. In a narrower sense this passage becomes a defense for remaining unmarried. *Cf.* Corinthians I, 7,8. St. Matthew 19,10. etc.

69. S. K. here characterized his suffering (illness or visitation) as a disproportion between his soul and body which made it impossible for him to be like others, "realize the universal" [human lot]. For a time he was hoping to be cured and consulted a doctor, but when it was made clear to him that nothing could be done, he conceived of his "visitation" as "the thorn in the flesh" that crushed his human happiness, yes, but at the same time gave him a unique spiritual tensile strength, made him an exceptional being. Through it God educated him "privatissime" (No. 68) in order that he might teach others what God had taught him.

A thorn in the flesh: Paul used the expression (Cor. II, 12, 7) in connection with saying that he had received high revelations, but to prevent him from becoming a braggart, a thorn had been lodged in his flesh. S. K. interpreted this term as a reminder of Paul's life before his conversion, his *vita ante acta, cf.* No. 51 and note and No. 142.

Strength in weakness: Cor. II, 12, 9 (". . . for my strength is made perfect in weakness").

The girl's death: *Cf.* No. 51, section 6.

chase after the Un-Common, the Extra-Ordinary, as did the romanticists and as, in his earliest youth, S. K. himself felt tempted to do. *Cf.* No. 13.

70. *Peter*: suffered from melancholy like Søren and went through religious crises bordering on the morbid.
Sheherazade: of the Arabian Nights.

72. *Stages of Existence*: first described in *Either-Or*, later in *Stages on Life's Way* and—in very great detail—in *Concluding Unscientific Postscript*; moreover, in all of S. K.'s pseudonymous writings. The term "stage" is used in the sense of standpoint. Thus "Stages on Life's Way" indicates a description of various outlooks on life, e.g. the esthetic, the ethical and the religious, to which the *Postscript* adds the *confina* or border-areas such as irony (between the esthetic and the ethical) and humor (between the ethical and the religious).

judging. In his writings S. K. did not pronounce judgment on others, but his manner inferred a judgment of the contemporary age, an epigram on human beings.

maieutic (Greek: maieuomai=I deliver [like a midwife]). S. K. regarded his activity as maieutic, "helping to deliver," in the sense that he did not wish to agitate for Christianity, as he felt that each individual must be personally responsible for his relationsip to Christianity; but he felt he ought to create opportunities for others to take a standpoint by constantly endeavoring to present the Christian demand to them in its uncompromising purity and severity; then nobody could pretend to be ignorant of the meaning of true Christianity. This indirect method was what S. K. called maieutic, with a term that Socrates had used in the same sense when, by his indirect method of questioning without ever making any personal assertion, he "delivered" comprehension, helped others to understand his questions.

Made myself a stumbling-block: S. K. himself caused people to take offense at his writings.

Obedience . . . refers to Samuel I, 15, 22: "to hearken is better than the fat of rams."

Rewrites, etc.: copies, carbon copies, rough drafts.

Epigram: Here mainly in the sense of a witty, ironical remark.

73. *Socrates' words:* in pleading his own defense.

Schopenhauer, Arthur S. (1788-1860), German philosopher whose principal work "Die Welt als Wille und Vorstellung" (1819) expressed a pessimistic world outlook: the will to life, the vital urge that pervades everything and everybody also leads to everybody fighting everybody else, and a human being can avoid the hell of living only by repressing the vital urge. S. K. came to know S.'s philosophy toward the end of his life and —at a time when S. was completely unnoticed—K. was deeply captivated by his work, also in a purely artistic sense.

currente calamo: (Latin: curro=run and calamus= reed, pen; i.e., written rapidly).

74. κατ'εξοχήν (kat'exochèn): (Greek exoche=salient) by preference, in an eminent sense, *par excellence.*

A says—B agrees: In the introductory diapsalma in *Either-Or*, A. characterizes a creative writer as an unhappy being who deep in his heart conceals a great anguish and declares that he will rather be a swineherd than a creative writer (S. V. I, 3). B. enters into A's train of thought, but on ethical grounds (S. V. II, 188 f.) maintaining that a creative writer's ideal is always an untrue ideal, because a true ideal is always related to reality. S. K. here expresses the same idea when he says that an author only relates to the ideal in imagination and therefore does not feel obliged to live up to the ideals he presents in his books. In that sense both philosophers and clergymen are authors: they do not live up to their own precepts.

Witness to the Truth: Although S. K. here quite logically defines a witness to the truth as a being who in his personal life relates to the ideal (in contrast to writers and others who relate to the ideal in imagination), one finds in S. K. a growing tendency to identify a truth-witness with a *martyr*.

81. Schopenhauer used the term "peddlers of opinions" to describe journalists in "Die Welt als Wille und Vorstellung" Vol. 2, chapter 7.

82. *putting [guilt] at a distance by writing*: A basic concept of Goethe's as being the essence of creative and fictional writing. The quotation is from "Aus Meinem Leben. Dichtung und Wahrheit," Part II, Book 7.

83. *Either-Or*. This refers to the second edition issued in April 1849.

Victor Eremita: Cf. Chronological Survey, February 2, 1843.

87. *The matter of the hymn-book*: In 1844 a committee was formed to compile a new hymn-book (*cf.* VII[1] B 195, p. 379 and S. V. VII, 415, footnote).

"My heart now yearns . . .": A hymn by C. Knoll printed in *Kingo's Hymnbook for Church and Home*, No. 637.

88. *No man*: A pun on the writer *Ingemann's* name. *Ingen mand* means no man. Quotation from Act 2 of J. L. Heiberg's "Christmas Jokes and New Year's Jest."

89. *The Corsair*: A liberal periodical published by the Opposition 1840-46 and edited by Meïr Aaron Goldschmidt, 21, when the paper was founded. G. was a great admirer of S. K. and expressed this in a note about *Either-Or* in 1843; later, in 1845, he declared that when all other Danish writers were forgotten, the immortal

Victor Eremita would survive. S. K. who considered *The Corsair* as almost belonging to the Yellow Press felt uncomfortable at being praised in it and thought of publishing the note reproduced here, but abstained. However, in 1846, he was attacked in the Yearbook *Gaea* by the literary critic P. L. Møller who also worked on *The Corsair*. Thereupon S. K. under the pseudonym of "Frater Taciturnus" fired a violent counter-volley in the *Fædrelandet* ("The Fatherland") asking straight-out that he might be lambasted in *The Corsair*. His idea was in that way to afford Goldschmidt a chance of rehabilitating himself and getting out of the partnership with P. L. Møller. But G. chose to meet S. K.'s request for abuse, and, in a number of issues of *The Corsair*, delivered him up to ridicule in caricatures and captions.

The postscript: which was not included in the first printed edition is found in *The Papers* (IV B 59). Its final words express—ironically—a conception of existence as an old novel in which, to the reader's surprise, he constantly reads only of himself.

90. *"Two Eras"*: the title of Madame Gyllembourg's last short story (1845) in which she contrasted the period of the revolution with the 'forties. S. K. admired Madame G.'s works in which he found the vital nerve to be "a conscious welding together of great and small things, a tension between idyl and drama, the message that the decisive human conflicts are fought and settled within the framework of everyday life, and that this sphere, despite its confined scope, holds the ideal. For Madame G. does not, you know, represent daily life as being a contrast to the ideal; she sees the two elements bound up together in an insoluble union." (Elizabeth Hude: *Thomasine Gyllembourg and her Everyday Stories*, 1951, p. 328 f.) That was positing the problem in a way S. K. could accept, so in 1846 he wrote "A Literary Critique" about the story in question.

92. *But nothing must be written . . .* : S. K. decides
not to express himself directly on his conception of the
Corsair affair, as it would conflict with his Socratic
("maieutic") working method.

he turned to me . . . : Goldschmidt's conversations
with S. K. are reported in G.'s *Memories of My Life* (I,
275, f; 279 f; and 371 f).

Johannes Climacus: *Cf. Chronological Survey*, Feb.
27, 1846, and No. 176. *Frater Taciturnus*: *Cf.* note to No.
89.

95. *pereat*: He shall perish! Down with him!

96. *"North and South"*; A monthly which G. began to
edit in 1848.

absolute negativity: To S. K. who always regarded any
literary production as something that should represent
an idea, it was nonsensical and superficial to deal with a
thing like political opposition; on the contrary, he could
very well enjoy an authorship that in a purely nihilistic
vein aimed at achieving a negative attitude to life and
therefore criticized everything without exception.

the little article in "The Fatherland": S. K.'s article
about P. L. Møller, *cf.* the note to No. 89.

97. *Attacks of the rabble*: (*Cf.* Nos. 93-95 and 97).
These attacks helped S. K. make up his mind to continue
as a writer. The idea of seeking a parson's living he now
viewed as doubt of himself caused by his melancholy, a
melancholy aggravated by his having been able to live
on his private means, living in "the pure realms of the
mind and spirit" without any "bodily presuppositions,"
i.e. without having to earn his daily bread.

a melancholy idea: *Cf.* No. 90.

if I had not had private means: *Cf.* No. 67.

98. *Riegels, Horrebov, Boie, Riisbright*: Riegels was a
frivolous journalist and critic of the social order; the

three others were philosophers opposing Kant. Johannes Boye was the most outstanding, and his principal work "The Friend of the State" (1792) was the precursor of a kind of philosophy of evolution, that regarded concepts like justice and morality as dependent upon the regular evolution of culture. Consequently, he rejected Kant's ethics which sought to base justice and morality on pure reason.

Børge Riisbright also criticized Kant's doctrine on pure reason in a work published in 1803. In this he asserted the importance of pragmatic science as juxtaposed to Kant's critique of reason which only deals with the forms of our apprehension and thus is of a purely formal character.

99. *Shirked something*: played truant from reality.

100. *Kant*. In his "Kritik der Reinen Vernunft" [Critique of Pure Reason] (1781) Kant made apprehension (cognition) the object of profound analysis. He did not think we were able to apprehend the factual reality: "das Ding an sich," but only "die Erscheinungen": the external phenomena as they appear to our organs of cognition which are determined by our forms of cognition, the categories of the senses and of reason. Therefore he did not think that there necessarily was any conformity between the essence of our cognition and reality, "that there was reality in our thinking."

Hegel: Georg Wilhelm Friedrich H. (1770-1831) thought that by his philosophical system ("the system") he had overcome Kant's skepticism in regard to the possibilities of our cognition, our apprehension, as he boldly equated thinking with being; that is, he placed a sign of equation between the formations of our concepts and reality. That led him to the same conclusion as pre-Kantian philosophy had arrived at, viz., that there is "reality in our thinking"; but whereas the older philos-

ophers quite naïvely accepted this as a premise, as a fore-
gone conclusion, Hegel arrived at the same result "in a
deeper form," having thought the problem through and,
by way of his system, having found a means of over-
coming all the interior contrasts which, indeed, do crop
up. Hegel sees these contrasts as links in an evolutionary
process leading from spontaneous being (not a satisfying
form of existence) through a series of stages up to "absolute mind and spirit" which manifests itself sensually in
art, emotionally in religion, and intellectually in "pure
thinking," which is life's highest goal and the highest
form of existence.

the preceding philosophers: this refers not only to
Kant's philosophy, but to all philosophies from the
dawn of time.

anthropological contemplation: consideration of human life, a rather unwieldy term for what S. K. later
called "the existential." (*Cf.* note to No. 57.) The old
philosophers who spontaneously took it for granted that
there was reality in thinking, had *time* to think existentially, whereas Hegel had to spend all his time proving
that thinking equalled being (*cf.* No. 101) and therefore
"only managed to arrive to the point, at which the philosophers of old started."

101. *Leibnitz*: German philosopher, about 1700, who
sought to unite a religious viewpoint with mechanical
physical science.

104. *Hegel . . . Christianity*: According to H. religion is
the second stage on the way toward absolute mind and
spirit, where one achieves comprehension of the Absolute
(God) in symbolic form. Through the various existing
religions the spiritual advances more and more, and at
the highest religious stage stands the true spiritual religion, the absolute religion: *Christianity*. Within Christianity itself a development also takes place tending toward

increasing spiritualization: from corroboration by way of external evidence and written works on faith to corroboration in the realm of pure thinking, which thus becomes the acme and final goal of Christianity. It is this fusion of religion and philosophy which S. K. calls "Reason's hypocrisy." Hegel "modified Christianity" by making it a philosophical movement and a link in his "system." S. K.'s great controversy with the Hegelian philosophy is presented in *"Concluding Unscientific Postscript."*

105. *The Trinity*: According to Hegel God or the Absolute is divided in three parts since the spirit must first be seen *"an sich"* as the eternal God-idea, as a unit in pure thinking (=the Father); then as the spirit in its varied multiplicity in relation to reality, God's existence as physical nature (=the Son); and finally the spirit's reverting to itself in the minds and consciences of the believers (=the Holy Ghost).

106. *a place in my dissertation*: S. V. XIII, 310. *Cf.* also *Chronological Survey*—Sept. 29, 1841.

107. *Easter Morning*: "When on the return trip I [J. L. Heiberg] now decided to stay over in Hamburg . . . it so happened that one day (as I was sitting in my room in the "König von England" with Hegel before me on my desk and Hegel in my mind, and at the same time listening to the fine hymns that almost constantly could be heard from the Petri church choir) I suddenly—in a manner that I have never experienced before or later— had a momentary inner vision like a flash of lightning that suddenly illuminated the whole sphere for me and revealed Hegel's hitherto concealed central idea. From that moment the system became clear to me in its general lines, and I was completely convinced that I had grasped its innermost core." J. L. Heiberg: *"Autobiographical Fragments"* (Prose Writings XI, 500).

Leaps. Heiberg, on the basis of his Hegelian logic,

maintained that leaps did not occur in the life of the mind and spirit; there everything was subject to continuous evolution, "transitions" brought about by way of "meditation," i.e. reconciling or leveling out contrasts. Against this view S. K. posits *the leap*, which assumes passion, as being the momentum that may explain the motion in our human existence.

108. *his outcry*: Heiberg reviewed *Either-Or* in his periodical *"Intelligensblade,"* No. 24 (March 1, 1843).

110. *New Year's present*: "Urania. Yearbook 1844, edited by I. L. Heiberg" presented an article "The astronomical year" with, *inter alia*, a misunderstood review of S. K.'s: *"The Repetition."* Astronomy was Heiberg's hobby.

114. *The bad Infinity*: A concept of Hegel's. He makes a distinction between a good and a bad Infinity. Good Infinity is present when the concept is dominated by the idea and by dialectics is able to carry thought progressively forward to some new content. Bad Infinity is present when an exchange of thoughts leads into an endless series of uniform links that are incapable of carrying the thought process forward to some new content. In such a case thought is blocked, can neither progress, nor form any new syntheses.

Bad Infinity occurs when Infinity is mistaken for Endlessness. The latter is the product of a simple addition of "finite-nesses." Therefore, there can, at most, be question of a bad or a negative Infinity; for the *finite has to end* some time, but Infinity cannot bring it about, for it has no hold on itself. Endlessness may be visualized as a straight line, that may be endlessly prolonged, prolonged *ad libitum*, whereas good (true) Infinity finds expression in the circle. Stethoscopy, like any other scientific invention, to S. K. represented "bad Infinity,"

i.e. it stands for an endless series of inventions which all
have this in common that they do not lead to anything
higher, they do not lead to any new ethical or religious
conception.

About bad Infinity *I. L. Heiberg* wrote: "What Hegel
calls the bad Infinity is what one usually imagines as
the infinite, the eternal itself in its unlimited extension.
On the contrary, the good (true) Infinity does not appear
in the form of external extension, but is concentrated
upon itself and is eternally present. This is the Infinity
the contents of which is held within a circle that runs
back into itself, wherein nothing is permanently or in-
alterably fixed as beginning or end, cause or effect, means
or purpose, subject or object, and so on; in brief, in
which no final decision remains firm and unshakeable,
but dissolves and merges into its own contrast. . . . Infinity, in other words, means everything that is idea and
idea is everything in which the non-factual is the real."
("*Critique of Dr. Rothe's doctrine on the Trinity and
Atonement*," 1837, *Prose Writings*, II, 28 f.)

When most people get caught in the error of mistak-
ing infinity for endlessness it is because they have not yet
progressed to *reflection*, but have remained in the sphere
of *spontaneity*, and therefore never consciously have realized their basis; (i.e. the foundation and origin of their
existence, *cf.* Heiberg's "Writings" I, 169) nor their
prius (i.e. their lives as links in a chain, in other words,
as belonging to both the past and the future). For this
reason the dialectical process is not set going, and a
person who remains in the sphere of spontaneity will
never rise out of it and, therefore, will remain in his
bad Infinity (*cf.* Note to No. 100 on Hegel).

Heiberg gave an idea of the meaning of bad Infinity
in Act 3 of his verse drama "A Soul after Death," when
his Mephistopheles says: [in unrhymed translation]

> If you comprehended philosophy,
> I easily could explain it:
> Our sphere is plain spontaneity
> which no eternity ever sets free,
> for it has no deeper foundation;
> and having no "Prius," no lasting relation,
> it is doomed to remain what it always was . . .

Stethoscope: Tube for listening to the lungs and the heart constructed by the Frenchman Laennec in 1819.

116. *qualitative dialectics*: Investigation of the value of things in an ethical as against a quantitative sense, the latter relating to amounts and dimensions. The concept of *approximation*, of the "Almost," with S. K. has a basic meaning in principle, as he believes that all natural, as well as historical, science only represents approximations and not true cognition.

117. "Go to the Devil knows where in the arse" is a term borrowed from Ludvig Holberg [the Danish Molière] who uses an equivalent in "*The Political Tinker*" Act V, Scene 2, and something on the same order in "*Jean de France*," Act I, Scene 1.

119. *Freedom*, i.e. free will. To S. K. "free will" meant freedom to "choose for one's self" or, in one's choice between good and evil to be capable of choosing "good." In other words, to him freedom denotes the possibility of living a moral life according to ethico-religious principles. So freedom is not just the ability to choose between good and bad, but being capable of choosing "good"—or of not choosing anything at all. (*Cf. The Concept of Dread*, S. V. IV, 320, 380 f.)

Necessity. S. K. in other words was not an unqualified adherent of the hypothesis of free will, *liberum arbitrium*, unlimited arbitrary freedom of choice. For whoever failed to make a determined choice of "good" would fall under the law of necessity, i.e. causality. Freedom includes a possibility of eventual change; necessity (causality) is what it is and remains so for ever; it is the unalterable, the eternal. It lies in the nature of things that the scientist must deal with causality; hence he can never apprehend actions conditioned by free will and so it will always fall to his lot to deal with matters that, from an ethical and religious viewpoint, are of no importance. S. K.'s aversion to the natural sciences was a result of this line of thinking. To him they belonged to the sphere of the bad Infinity.

121. *Phantoms and make-believe of objectivity*: All through his life S. K. was fighting to tear off the mask of false objectivity wherewith not least Hegelian philosophy camouflaged concepts like the state, the community, the people, the nation, public affairs, "the public," etc. Since the most important thing to S. K. was to make people aware of the Christian choice that confronted them through the alternatives inherent in "free will" (*cf.* note on freedom, No. 119) and to tear them away from the bad Infinity, it was necessary for him to stress the significance of having faith in one's own subjectivity. "As soon as subjectivity is taken away, and from subjectivity: passion, and from passion: its infinite interest, then there is no decision left to make, neither about this, nor about any other problem. All decision, all essential decision, rests on subjectivity." (*Concluding Unscientific Postscript*, S. V. V, VII, 21.)

The category of the individual: With S. K. the separate individual is a basic concept—a category. He sees the individual as the true presupposition of all religiosity. The individual is in the category of spiritual awakening, and with the individual stands or falls the cause of Christianity at a time when the evolution of the world has advanced so far in reflection as is now the case, and Christianity is running the risk of losing itself in pantheism and abstract speculation. (See more on this subject under No. 122.)

122. *Evolution tends to* . . . The trend of world evolution is tending increasingly toward philosophizing, abstractions and generalizations about ordinary concepts, "the phantoms of objectivity." But that is precisely the reason why the category of the individual becomes so desperately important.

Concretely—in abstracto: Not admitted in concrete cases, though admitted in a general way.

Bishop Møller: Rasmus Møller, d. 1842, was Poul Møller's father. As bishop of the diocese of Lolland-Falster he wrote: "Guidance to intelligent and devotional reading of the New Testament, especially for non-learned readers."

126. *Ataraxia*: (Greek: tarasso=disturb); imperturbability, complete tranquillity of mind.

eo ipso: precisely because of that.

132. *Goethe, cf.* No. 82.

137. *second power of dialectics*: i.e. first, as a thinking, secondly, as an existing being.

It is this repetition of the imagined twofold movement in life which S. K. describes by the term: to *reduplicate*: to make double. *Cf.* the beginning of No. 142 where the idea is given its simplest definition.

139. in a different category from the universal [the ordinary, common lot]: S. K. distinguished between artists and scientists, who differ from the general run of mankind by virtue of their extraordinary talents, and therefore may claim *admiration*, and ethical persons who "realize the universal" and whose lives consequently constitute a claim on their fellow-men to live likewise. This claim may be advanced because, in contrast to the "different" artists and scientists, it does not presuppose or need any kind of extraordinary talent. Anyone may

realize such an existence, but it is precisely this "claim" or demand that *arouses the anger of the crowd.*

140. Bombazine: a material made of wool and silk.

144. *Irony* was a concept that occupied S. K. all his life. It was the subject of his dissertation and later became an important ingredient in his thinking processes (*cf.* "*Postscript*" second edition, A. par. 3 [S. V. VII, 436 ff.]).

In a general sense, irony marks a lack of accordance between what is uttered and what is meant, yet in such a way that the door is left ajar for people to get an inkling of what the speaker or writer actually means. In other words, a man who expresses himself ironically is more or less hiding his real opinions; that is why S. K. calls irony an "*incognito.*" But why would a person need an "*incognito*"? Because it is not possible to expound Christianity directly, nor to preach about ethical conduct, because both presuppose that the preacher reduplicates his preaching [practices what he preaches]; but who can say about himself that he fulfills the claims of Christianity or even of ethics? Not S. K. (*cf.* for instance the beginning of No. 142). Just therefore he must use the *incognito* of irony; it enables him to express what he has in mind without direct preaching and also without being liable to the reproach that he fails to practice what he preaches.

Thus irony includes ethical earnestness, but actually does not become irony until it is put up against conventional culture and its conventional expression, even to the extent that nobody notices the irony. "Nobody," however, must be taken with a grain of salt, since the intention of irony is to lead the reflective mind forward, induce it to comprehend by "the maieutic method." But since that will apply only to a minority—and actually would confuse the majority—an ironic person is always unpopular (No. 145). Irony was used consistently for the first time in the service of a higher purpose by Socrates, who wished to arouse his audience to independent thinking. Hence his talks often ended without any conclusion being drawn, but leaving a sting. (No. 146.)

147. *Bileam's ass*: God conferred upon it the gift of being able to talk to its master. (Fourth Book of Moses —called Numbers—22, 28.)

151. *quoad doctrinam*: in respect to his teaching.
difference (the): Cf. No. 139 and note.

160. *Themistocles*: According to Plutarch Themistocles was so apt at putting himself in the place of Miltiades that *he* later was able to save the Greeks in the battle of Salamis, just as Miltiades, ten years earlier, had saved them in the battle of Marathon.

161. *Bernard*: The episode is based on Fr. Böhringer's account of "Die Kirche Christi und ihre Zeugen oder die Kirchengeschichte in Biographien" (1842-49) Vol. 2, Sect. 1, p. 527. [The Church of Christ and its Witnesses, or Church-History by way of Biographies.]
man's brute destiny: Cf. Nos. 124 and 125.

164. *married*: Regine Olsen was married to Johan Friederich Schlegel on Nov. 3, 1847.

169. *The Communist rebellion*: The February revolution in France and its repercussions in Europe. The term "Communism" was used by several political factions in the 'forties, but it received a more precise definition by the Communist Manifesto which Marx and Engels elaborated about the end of 1847.

170. *the last book*, i.e. *Christian Discourses by S. Kierkegaard. Anders*: S. K.'s man-servant was drafted for military service at the outbreak of the Dano-Prussian war.
the new book about the Sickness unto Death: Cf. *Chronological Survey*, July 30, 1849.

174. *Strube*: A joiner-journeyman who resided with S. K. in the apartment at the corner of Rosenborggade and Tornebuskegade and went insane from religious brooding.

income tax: Up until 1848 income tax had been known only very intermittently, but during the 3-years' war (between Germany and Denmark) it was introduced as a temporary measure. But in many quarters it was considered expedient to make it permanent, and a bill to that effect was introduced in the 1850-51 budget by Finance Minister Sponneck.

Reitzel: Carl Andreas R. (1787-1853), a Danish publisher who succeeded in having most of the important Danish authors on his list.

175. *I cannot*: i.e. go on expounding Christianity directly through my writings, as a witness to the Truth, S. K. felt.

The journal NB[10]: S. K. numbered his diaries and preserved them carefully.

Reflection incarnate: always "in reverse," thinking back. *Cf.* No. 136.

Admit my activity: i.e. openly acknowledge all his writings including those published pseudonymously. S. K. had written a pamphlet with this eventuality in view: "The viewpoint for my work as an author," wherein for the first time, he spoke directly about his purpose as a writer. At that time he was greatly torn by doubts as to whether he should publish the book, but he finally decided against it. It was published posthumously.

176. The other thing: i.e. to act by stepping forward as the *extra-ordinary* man and preach Christianity. S. K. held back, because he essentially regarded himself as "a poet" who presented the Christian demands without people having the right to demand "reduplication" of him. He vacillated between three eventualities: 1) termi-

nating his authorship ("in character"=officially) and stepping forward as a preacher; 2) terminating his authorship and seeking office; 3) continuing his writing—but as things were developing he would be deprived of the necessary economic basis for that.

Demoniacal: in S. K.'s conception this was a special form of dread, i.e. dread of the Good. The demoniacal would prevail when a human being had sunk so deeply into sin that it no longer tried to resist, no longer even wishes to be free of it, but prefers to remain in unfreedom, in sin (*cf.* the notes to No. 119 on "freedom" and "necessity"). It is characteristic of a demoniacal person that he isolates himself in reserve. (*Cf. The Concept of Dread*, Chap. IV, par. 2, Dread of the Good, S. V. IV, 386 ff.)

the "Interesting": The age was much occupied with this concept as against earlier Romanticism's more naive cultivation of the Fine and the Good. The age sought a combination of romanticism and realism and wanted artistic elaboration of phenomena, psychologically more complicated than earlier authors had offered. S. K. presented the Interesting as a special category: "The Interesting is a category that, mainly in our age, and precisely because the age is *in discrimine rerum* (at a turning point in history) has gained great importance, for it is actually the very category of the turning point. . . . At least it is certain that to become interesting, or to make one's life interesting, is not a task for arts-and-crafts, but a fateful privilege that, like every privilege in the world of mind and spirit, may be bought only at the price of deep anguish." (*Fear and Trembling*, S. V. III, 131. *Cf.* also No. 74.)

177. *de se ipso*: about myself.

Here lies the burden of my concluding postscript: "*Concluding Unscientific Postscript*" (for full title see *Chronological Survey* for Feb. 27, 1846) is a postscript to

"Philosophical Bits" which deals philosophically with the problem of Christianity. Its detailed character is more specifically described on the title page: "Can there be a historical point of departure for eternal consciousness, and, if so, can such a point present more than merely historical interest; can eternal salvation be based on an item of historical knowledge?" In this work S. K. succeeded in giving a definition of all the basic Christian concepts: sin, grace, God incarnated, God as a savior, redeemer and atoner; the paradox, faith and scandal.

"The Postscript" is a postscript insofar as it deals with a problem that is necessary for putting everything in the right perspective: i.e. the problem about subjectivity, the individual by himself—how do *I* become a Christian? It is quite impossible to gain objective knowledge of what Christianity is; everything depends upon one's personal appropriation of it. It is the degree of inwardness and passion that determines whether one is a true Christian or not. Truth then is subjective, nay, subjectivity is truth ("the suffering in inwardness attendant upon becoming a Christian"). Therein lies the understanding of the expressions "to lose one's reason" (for truth is inaccessible to objective, i.e. intellectual apprehension) and "crucified to the paradox" (which means that since truth cannot be apprehended objectively, but only through deep, subjective passion, it must appear to the apprehending subject as being outside the pale of the intellectual categories, in other words, as being a paradox). S. K.'s thoughts on this pivotal subject are expressed in their most concentrated form in the last chapter of the Postscript. (S. V. VII, 511 ff., especially 532 f.)

183. *The Collected Works of Consummation.* At one time S. K. was planning to collect his as yet unpublished works which included *"The Sickness unto Death"* and issue them in one volume under the above-mentioned title, and thereupon terminate his writing career.

189. *Spontaneity.* A term borrowed from Hegel meaning the opposite of reflection. In the present context it refers to the state in which, like Adam and Eve in the Garden of Eden, one is unaware of the difference between good and evil, and therefore has no consciousness of sin, nor feeling of guilt. Hence, also a state of innocence like that of a small child. So consciousness of sin becomes a phase of reflection that assumes capability of distinguishing between good and evil. Only as a person becomes conscious of sin does the former state of spontaneity and innocence, whose essence is ignorance, explode.

Mind-and-Spirit. S. K. distinguished between soul and mind-and-spirit. The physical-psychical is the animal or vegetative part which is subject to natural causality; mind-and-spirit lives in the sphere of free will and is capable of making ethico-religious decisions, in part independently of the psychical-physical constitution. One becomes mind-and-spirit by believing in the forgiveness of sin.

190. *What kind of spontaneity?* Through the absurd belief in the forgiveness of sin man again achieves a kind of new spontaneity, an acquired spontaneity, that, however, differs from his original spontaneity which with its ignorance and selfishness is lost for ever.

193. *Kant's theory*: In his "Religion innerhalb der Grenzen der blossen Vernunft" [Religion within the confines of pure reason] (1793) Kant sought to explain the fundamental imbalance in the human community, the radical evil, as being caused by men placing sensuality and egotism above moral norms. Still, he admits that he cannot quite understand the origin of radical evil and thus makes a *concession*, an admission, to the incomprehensible. However, S. K. did not wish to let it go at that; he wanted the incomprehensible, whittled into a

paradox (which would express the relation between the existing explorer, who can only apprehend piecemeal, and Eternal Truth), recognized as a special category of apprehension in the doctrine on the essence of things (ontology).

197. *First the kingdom of God*: Matthew 6,33.

198. *A blushing, oh Socrates, youth*: This may refer to Lysis in Platon's dialogue of the same name, a shy youth, but avid for knowledge. (See espec. 213 C.)

199. *historice*: in a historical sense. God is not a living reality, but a historical phenomenon.

exegetic and critical skepticism: this refers to the school of Bible critique that originated and grew in Germany among the so-called Young-Hegelians, especially *David Friedrich Strauss* whose *"Leben Jesu"* [Life of Jesus] (1835) regarded the Biblical accounts as more or less mythical, and *Ludwig Feuerbach* who in *"Das Wesen des Christenthums"* [The essence of Christianity] (1841) applied a psychological viewpoint to the Christian dogmas. Exegesis=interpretation, particularly of the Bible.

201. *one of the Diapsalmata*: S. V. I, 17.

Pathetic and dialectical transition: i.e. from one stage to another. Transition may either be dialectical, i.e. logically motivated, or pathetic (based on feeling) (*cf*. note to No. 98) which is the case of the living thinker.

The positive of saturation: the maximum attainable in a positive direction.

argumentum spiritus sancti: the testimony of the Holy Ghost.

209. S. K. used the Latin term *confinium*=border-area or limits.

made it a party matter: About 1525 Luther turned against the revolutionary peasants who had risen against their feudal lords, partly at the instigation of Luther himself, but later he threw himself into the arms of the princes.

212. *Apostle*: According to S. K.'s definition an apostle is a Christian who speaks with authority, i.e. one whom God has authorized to speak. Against the apostle he placed the genius, characterized by a wealth of innate talents, but who speaks without authority. S. K. regarded himself as a genius (No. 175) and his pseudonymous writings expressed just that. Nevertheless, many diary entries from his later years (*cf.* No. 177) show that he devoted a great deal of thought to the possibility that he might have a special mission and consequently also would have authority. However, he never used the term "apostle" about himself, though he did strive to become a witness to Truth (*cf.* Nos. 211 and 219). He distinguished between three categories of Christians: 1) the apostles; 2) the witnesses to Truth; 3) the teachers of religion, i.e. the clergy. The witnesses to Truth were those who realized their teaching in their own lives and were marked by suffering for the sake of Christ's gospel. (X^3 A 570). *Cf.* S. K.'s dissertation "*On the difference between a genius and an apostle*" (1849) in "*Two minor ethico-religious dissertations.*" S. V. XI.

Luther's formula. By declaring: "I cannot do otherwise," Luther asserted that he acted from necessity (causality), thereby disavowing free will which offers the possibility of a choice, and which is the presupposition of Christianity (*cf.* Nos. 227 and 239).

Diagnostician: he who makes a diagnosis (Greek: diagnosis=distinction, definition of the nature of an illness). S. K. especially wished to be active as a diagnostician (*cf.* note for No. 60).

The sickness: The ailments of Christendom. *Cf.* "*The Sickness unto Death.*"

213. Proclaiming the "Apostle": who preferred to stress Mercy where Christ puts forth the demand of emulation [Imitation of Christ]. S .K. was originally a Luther enthusiast, but gradually waxed more and more critical of him. S. K.'s ever stricter Christian demands also led him to turn against the apostle Paul.

214. *"The professor"* in S. K.'s mind came to represent the dispassionate, "objective," non-existential thinker who will construct systems and thinks he can understand what lies "beyond reason," the paradoxical. When S. K. ironically characterized "the professor" as "Evolution's finest and richest flower" it involved an allusion to Hegel's system which culminated in "pure thinking."

216. "of sixteen summers": This is in quotation marks because S. K. was quoting from his own book "Stages on Life's Way," (S. V. VI, 247).

226. *Mynster,* Jacob Peter, born 1775; from 1802 pastor in the rural parish of Spiellerup near Fakse (Sealand), and from 1834 Bishop of Sealand. In his mind a pietistic trend mingled with an urge to absorb the romantic cultural life of the times. On this basis he became the originator of the so-called "parsonage-culture" that flourished in Denmark in the 19th century. As a rural vicar he became used to solitude, and he cultivated the custom of having quiet devotional moments in church as well as in private prayer at home. (*Cf.* No. 226.) In Spiellerup he also learned to speak simply and unaffectedly on sacred matters, though by no means without artistic skill. (Nos. 219 and 228.)

As a thinker he stressed religion and faith as natural human drives and, therefore, as natural links in general culture along with other cultural forms, such as arts and sciences (No. 227). However, he disagreed with the Hegelian philosophy and its idea that it could reconcile and align all contrasts in life, thereby making Christianity a link in a system, and in a pamphlet entitled "Super-

Naturalism-Rationalism" (1839) he maintained that it
was necessary to choose between two alternatives: either
belief in the divine or in the rational, and he confronted
his opponents with an "Either-Or"!

The importance of Mynster to S. K. was vast. Already
the old Kierkegaard was deeply influenced by Mynster,
and S. K. was aware of both the pietistic and the cultural
urge in his own nature. From Mynster he learned style
as well as mode of expression, and he carried on Mynster's controversy against Hegelianism with its levelling
of contrasts, right down to adopting the term *Either-Or*.
Only in the last years of his life (from about 1848) did
S. K. become truly critical of Mynster's Christianity with
its life-confirming and culture-confirming characteristics.
Virtuosity à la Goethe: Cf. No. 82.

227. In this entry S. K. accepts Luther's statement as
denoting a true choice. Six years later (*cf*. No. 212) he
rejected it as constituting a denial of free will, thereby
assuming as critical an attitude toward Luther as, in
1848, toward Mynster.

Mynster's sermon: In "Sermons on all Sundays and
Holy Days during the Year" (Third edition 1837).

229. *"a man clothed in soft raiment"*; Matthew 11,8.
the demoniacal: Cf. the note to No. 176.

231. *Martensen*, Hans Lassen M. (1808-74) was influenced by Sibbern and Mynster; he was a friend of J. L.
Heiberg and, like him, since 1834 an adherent of the
Hegelian philosophy. He tutored in theology; after Poul
Møller's death in 1838 he became assistant professor of
philosophy, and in 1849 professor of theology. In 1854
he succeeded Mynster as Bishop of Sealand. He wanted
to overcome "the subjectivity inherent in the romantic
morality" by "a theoretical apprehension of objectivity,
of the finite form of the state, of religion, science and
art." His theological writings which in the 'thirties and

'forties had been following a preponderantly inquiring, philosophical trend, culminated with "Christian Dogmatics" (1849) in which he classified all Christian concepts, right down to the order of precedence of angels.

S. K., who in his freshman year was tutored by Martensen, always felt contempt for him; his "assurances," i.e. his authoritative, didactic method was utterly different from S. K.'s own indirect, dialectical method, and he regarded Martensen as a typical "professor" (*cf.* No. 214 and note).

indulge: Here "to indulge science" means to S. K.: in peace and quiet to potter about with detailed, scientific problems (e.g. the bad Infinity; *cf.* note to No. 114).

233. *I expressed my disagreement through my pseudonyms*: especially Johannes Climacus in "Postscript" where the "Privat-Dozent" (assistant professor) constantly figures. (*Cf.* No. 98.)

A small rap: In the foreword to his "Dogmatics" Martensen mentioned "certain others" (i.e., S. K.) "who are capable of thinking only in glimpses, notions, apothegms [desultory ideas]."

235. *Now he is dead*: Mynster died on January 30, 1854.

"the desperate thing in connection with Goldschmidt": In a book Mynster had praised S. K. (*cf. Chronological Survey*, March 13, 1851) by using an expression of "one of our most talented authors" i.e. Goldschmidt. This made a most painful impression on S. K., for two reasons: First, to see Goldschmidt, an individual whom he himself rejected as not up to par, being accepted by Mynster; secondly, to be mentioned in connection with him. (*Cf. Chronological Survey*, March 13, 1851.)

Kolthorf: Minister at the Church of the Holy Ghost in Copenhagen.

236. "The Outcry": "But at midnight there was a cry

made" (Matthew 25,6). This was used as a quotation on the title page of the pamphlet entitled *"This must be said: so let it then be said,"* wherein S. K. declared that public worship in the churches was tantamount to blasphemy.

The article against Martensen: Cf. *Chronological Survey*, Dec. 18, 1854.

Countess Orsini: In Lessing's "Emilia Galotti," Act 4, Scene 5.

238. *Doubts*: Defined in the "Postscript" as "the reaction against the absolute relation's absolute expression" and "the resistance inherent in the Absolute" (S. V. VII, 400). S. K. conceived of doubt as an illness emanating from the divinity itself, whereby the latter repels the finite being. Doubt manifests itself as religious fear, a fear of the Good, based on the individual relating itself absolutely to the relative (the multiple facets of life) and resisting, as long as possible, recognition of the Absolute (God) in its absolute expression (i.e. His unconditional demands).

Scandal: "If paradox and reason collide in a common understanding of their differences, the collision is happy like the understanding between two lovers . . . If the collision fails in understanding, the relationship is unhappy and this: reason's unhappy love . . . we might, with a more precise term, call "Scandal" [we take offense at it; feel scandalized]. (*Philosophical Bits* [Fragments]; S. V. IV, 215 f.) In other words, the risk of scandal lies in reason taking offense at the fact that there is something which is outside its competence ("beyond reason" or intelligence) i.e. the paradoxical.

239. *Most human beings*: S. K. distinguished in the following among three categories of men: 1) those bereft of spirituality, whose lives are so empty that punishment will not apply to them, wherefore they are lost; 2) those

who eventually may receive mercy and be brought to *taedium vitae* [become utterly fed up with life], but who are scandalized and rebel against God; 3) those who, likewise brought to *taedium vitae,* maintain that God acts as He does from love. Only the last are ripe for eternal life.

can be accomplished only in freedom: By free will. (*Cf.* No. 212 and note—Luther's formula.)

CHRONOLOGICAL SURVEY

1796	3/23	Michael Pedersen Kierkegaard's first wife died.
1797	4/26	M. P. K. married Ane Sørensdatter Lund.
—	7/7	Birth of their first child.
1813	5/5	S. K. was born.
1821		S. K. entered "Borgerdydskolen" (a well-known boys' school in Copenhagen).
1830		S. K. matriculated at the university of Copenhagen.
1834		S. K.'s mother died.
—		S. K. was tutored by H. L. Martensen.
1836–37		S. K. attended Poul Møller's lectures on the general concepts of metaphysics. S. K.'s period of dissipation.
1837	5/8	S. K. on his way to call on Bolette Rørdam, but turned round and went home. (No. 47.)
—	5/9	S. K. met Regine Olsen at the Rørdams' (No. 48.)
—	July	S. K. moved from his father's home.
—	/7	S. K. moved from his father's home. Attended H. L. Martensen's lectures on an approach to dogmatics.
1838	3/13	Poul Møller died (Nos. 57–58.)
—	8/8	S. K.'s father died (No. 37) "The big earthquake" (Nos. 38, 41).
—	9/7	*From the Papers of one still living* was published.
1840	7/3	Passed his final theological examination (No. 51).

— **7/19**–8/6 Pilgrimage to Saedding (Nos. 42-43).
— 9/8 S. K. proposed to Regine (No. 51).
— 9/10 Regine accepted him (No. 51).
1841 8/11 S. K. returned her ring.
— 9/29 Defended hs dissertation *"On the Concept of Irony, with constant regard to Socrates."*
— 10/11 Final break with Regine (No. 51).
— 10/25 Trip to Berlin (No. 56).
1842 3/6 S. K. returned from Berlin.
1843 2/20 *"Either-Or. A Fragment of Life edited by Victor Eremita"* was published.
— 5/8 Second trip to Berlin.
— 5/16 *"Two Edifying Discourses by S. Kierkegaard"* was published (No. 61).
— 10/16 *"Fear and Trembling. Dialectic Lyrics by Johannes de Silentio,"* was published.
— — *"Repetition. An attempt at experimental Psychology by Constantin Constantius"* was published.
— — *"Three Edifying Discourses by S. Kierkegaard"* was published.
— 12/6 *"Four Edifying Discourses by S. Kierkegaard"* was published.
— 6/19 The "Urania" Yearbook for 1843, edited by I. L. Heiberg was issued (No. 110). In the article "The Astronomical Year" S. K.'s *"Repetition"* was mentioned.
1844 3/5 *"Two Edifying Discourses by S. Kierkegaard"* was published.
— 6/8 *"Three Edifying Discourses by S. Kierkegaard"* was published.
— 6/13 *"Philosophical Bits, [Fragments] or a Bit of Philosophy by Johannes Climacus,"* edited by S. Kierkegaard, was published.
— 6/17 *"The Concept of Dread. A Simple Psycho-*

logically-directed Deliberation on the Dogmatic Problem concerning Original Sin by
Vigilius Haufniensis" was published.

— — "Foreword. Entertaining Reading for Certain Classes according to Time and Opportunity by Nicolaus Notabene," was published.

— 8/31 "Four Edifying Discourses by S. Kierkegaard" was published.

1845 4/29 "Three Addresses on Fictive Occasions by
S. Kierkegaard" was published.

— 4/30 "Stages on Life's Way. Studies by Various
Persons, brought into Print and Edited by
Hilarius Bookbinder," was published.

— 5/13 Third trip to Berlin.

— 5/29 "Eighteen Edifying Discourses by S. Kierkegaard" was published.

— 12/22 "GÆA, Esthetic Yearbook for 1846, edited
by P. L. Møller" (with a review of "Stages
on Life's Way") was published.

— 12/27 In an article in "Fædrelandet" (The Fatherland) Frater Taciturnus expressed a wish to
be lambasted in "The Corsair" (No. 89).

1846 1/2 First article in "The Corsair" about S. K.,
with a caricature.

— 2/7 S. K.'s thoughts on terminating his writing
career and becoming a minister (No. 90).

— 2/27 "Concluding Unscientific Postscript to 'Philosophical Bits.' Mimic-pathetic-dialectical
Miscellany, an existential plea* by Johannes
Climacus, edited by S. Kierkegaard," was
published.

— 3/30 A Literary Review. "Two Eras," Short story
by the author of "An Everyday-Story," reviewed by S. Kierkegaard, was published.
(No. 90.)

—	10/2	Goldschmidt resigns from his editorial post with "The Corsair."
1847	3/13	*"Edifying Discourses with different approaches, by S. Kierkegaard"* was published.
—	9/29	*"The Works of Love. Christian Deliberations in the guise of Discourses by S. Kierkegaard"* was published.
—	11/3	Regine was married to Fritz Schlegel (No. 164).
—	12/23	Goldschmidt started the periodical "Nord og Syd" ("North and South") (No. 96).
1848	4/19	S. K. had certain spiritual and psychological experiences followed by talks with his doctor. (No. 165.)
—	4/26	*"Christian Discourses by S. Kierkegaard"* was published.
—	4/–	S. K. moved into an apartment at Torne-buskegade, 156, (Nos. 170 and 174).
—	3/23	Outbreak of the Dano-Prussian Three-Years' War. (No. 169.)
—	7/24–27	*"The Crisis and a Crisis in the Life of an Actress by Inter-Inter,"* four articles in "The Fatherland."
—	11/–	S. K. finished *Viewpoint for my Activity as a Writer. A Direct Communication, a Report to History*; but he decided not to publish it. (Nos. 170 and 175.)
1849	2/–	The idea of Martyrdom began to occur to S. K. (No. 177.)
—	5/14	Second edition of *Either-Or* appeared. (No. 83.)
—	—	*"The Lilies of the Field and the Birds of the Air.* Three devotional discourses by S. Kierkegaard,"* was published.

* Translator's Note: Reference to Matthew 6,26 where "birds" is given as "fowl." 6:28: "Consider the lilies of the field . . . the fowl of the air . . ."

—	—	*"Two/ethico-religious treatises by H. H."* was published.
1849	6/25	State Councilor Olsen died. (No. 174.)
—	7/19	"Christian Dogmatics. Presented by Dr. H. Martensen," was published (Nos. 231-33).
—	7/30	*"The Sickness unto Death. A Christian-psychological exposition for edification and awakening by Anti-Climacus, edited by S. Kierkegaard,"* was published. (Nos. 170 and 176.)
—	11/13	*"The High Priest—the Publican—and the Woman taken in Sin; three addresses at Holy Communion on Fridays by S. Kierke-gaard,"* was published.
1850	9/27	*"Training in Christianity by Anti-Climacus, Nos. I, II, III, edited by S. Kierkegaard,"* was published. (No. 176.)
—	12/20	*"An Edifying Discourse by S. Kierkegaard"* was published.
1851	3/13	"Further contributions to the deliberations on ecclesiastical conditions in Denmark" with remark about S. K. and Goldschmidt, by Mynster, was published. (No. 238.)
—	7/7	*"On my Activity as a Writer by S. Kierke-gaard"* was published.
—	—	*"Two discourses at Holy Communion on Fridays by S. Kierkegaard"* was published.
—	9/10	*"For Self-Testing. Recommended to the Contemporary Age by S. Kierkegaard,"* was published.
1854	1/30	Bishop Mynster died. (No. 235.)
—	4/15	Martensen was appointed bishop.
—	12/18	Article by S. K. in "The Fatherland": *Was Bishop Mynster* "a Witness to the Truth," one of "the true Witnesses to the Truth"

		—is this the truth? The first of 21 articles in "The Fatherland."
1855	5/24	*This Must be Said; Then Let it be Said. By S. Kierkegaard.* ("The Outcry," cf. No. 236.)
—	—	The first number of "Ojeblikket" (The Moment) was published.
—	6/16	*"Christ's Judgment on Official Christianity,"* was published.
—	9/3	*"God's Unchangeability. A Discourse"* was published.
—	9/25	No. 9 of "Ojeblikket" (the Moment) was issued.
—	—	S. K.'s last Journal-entry (No. 239).
—	10/2	S. K. was hospitalized at Frederiks Hospital, Copenhagen.
—	11/11	S. K. died.

COMPARATIVE INDEX

Nos. 1-239 indicate the numbering of the entries in the present book. The symbols facing these numbers indicate the sources from which the entries were drawn in *Kierkegaard's Papers* ("Søren Kierkegaards Papirer"—original Danish marking).

BRIEF BIBLIOGRAPHY

S. K.'s Works

Samlede Værker [Collected Works]: First edition 1901-06.
Vols. I-XIV. Second edition 1920-36. Vols. I-XV.
The last vol. contains subject and author index
and a terminological index by J. Himmelstrup.

Søren Kierkegaards Papirer [S. K.'s Papers], 20 vols. 1909-
1948.

P. V. Rubow: Kierkegaard-Manuskripter (Danske Digtere
ved Arbejdet) [S. K. Manuscripts (Danish Writers
at Work)] 1935.

F. Brandt: Kierkegaards udødelige Tanker (Udødelige
Tanker No. 12) [S. K.'s immortal Thoughts (in the
series Immortal Thoughts No. 12)] 2 vols. 2nd ed.
1950.

F. J. Billeskov Jansen: Søren Kierkegaard. Indledninger
og Tekstforklaringer. [S. K. Selections from his
works with Introduction and commentaries] 4
vols. 1950.

Danish Works on S. K.

G. Brandes: Søren Kierkegaard. 1877.

H. Høffding: Søren Kierkegaard som Filosof [as a Philos-
opher] 1892.

E. Geismar: Søren Kierkegaard. 6 vols. 1926-28.

H. Helweg: Søren Kierkegaard. En psykiatrisk-psykolo-
gisk Studie. [A psychiatric-psychological study]
1933.

J. Hohlenberg: Søren Kierkegaard, 1940.
——. Den ensommes Vej. En fremstilling af S. K.'s værk.
   [The Path of the Lonely One. An account of S.
   K.'s Work] 1948.
F. J. Billeskov Jansen: Hvordan skal vi studere Søren
   Kierkegaard? (S. K. Selskabets populære Skrifter)
   [How shall we study S. K.? (A volume of the S. K.
   Society's popular documents)] 1949.
——. Studier i Søren Kierkegaards litterære Kunst.
   [Studies in S. K.'s literary art.] 1951.
Sejer Kühle: Søren Kierkegaard. Barndom og Ungdom.
   [Søren Kierkegaard. Childhood and Youth] 1950.